MW01206214

Quantum Creator

A Transformational Guide to Manifesting
with Thought, Energy & Identity

By Sage Yaz Hart

Copyright © 2025 Sage Yaz Hart

All rights reserved.

No part of this publication may be reproduced, distributed, or transmitted in any form or by any means; electronic, mechanical, photocopying, recording, or otherwise; without the prior written permission of the publisher, except in the case of brief quotations embodied in critical reviews and certain other noncommercial uses permitted by copyright law.

This book is a work of nonfiction and is intended to provide motivational and educational information. While every effort has been made to ensure accuracy, the author makes no guarantees and assumes no responsibility for any actions taken based on the content of this book.

For permissions or inquiries, contact:

yaz@sageyazhart.com

First Edition, 2025

ISBN:

Cover Design by: Independently published

Published by: Sage Yaz Hart

Printed/Distributed by: Amazon Kindle Direct Publishing (KDP)

Dedication

To the version of you that's still becoming.

The one who dreams, doubts, resets, and rises.

May this book remind you of what you already are:
powerful, whole, and profoundly capable of creating your own reality.

Acknowledgments

This book is the result of many unseen entanglements; of conversations, mentors, moments of inspiration, and divine nudges I could never fully explain.

To the quantum thinkers, the mystics, the scientists, and the spiritual rebels who have come before: thank you for illuminating the way.

To those who have supported my creative unfolding in silence or in presence, your energetic resonance shaped every page.

To the Source behind it all, who reminds me again and again: reality is not fixed. We are the field.

Author's Note

Dear Reader,

This is not just a book. It's a frequency.

A space for you to step into your next level of awareness, power, and embodiment.

You won't find formulas here, only frameworks. Not prescriptions, but portals.

Each chapter is an invitation to shift how you see yourself, your power, and the nature of reality itself.

Read slowly. Reflect often. Practice intentionally. Return as needed.

This book is meant to evolve with you.

You don't need to be a scientist to understand the universe.

You only need to remember: you are part of it.

With gratitude and resonance,

Sage Yaz Hart

Table of Contents

Dedication 3

Acknowledgments 4

Author's Note 5

Introduction 8

    Awaken the Quantum Creator Within 8

Chapter 1 13

    The Quantum Mind: Unlocking Your Thought Power 13

Chapter 2 26

    Wave-Particle Duality: Balancing Potential and Action 26

Chapter 3 38

    Superposition: The Infinite Possibilities of Being 38

Chapter 4 51

    The Observer Effect: Mindfulness for Success 51

Chapter 5 62

    Quantum Fields: The Science Behind the Law of Attraction 62

Chapter 6 75

    Entanglement: Embracing Universal Interconnectedness 75

Chapter 7 90

    The Uncertainty Principle: Thriving in the Unknown 90

Chapter 8 105

    Quantum Potentiality: Manifesting Dreams into Reality 105

Chapter 9 120

    Quantum Healing: Harnessing the Mind-Body Connection ... 120

Chapter 10 137

Quantum Coherence: Building a Harmonious Life......................137

Chapter 11 148

Quantum Timelines: Bending Time with Consciousness........148

Chapter 12 163

Quantum Leap: Transforming Your Life with Bold Change ...163

Chapter 13 173

The Multiverse: Exploring Infinite Possibilities.......................173

Chapter 14 (Bonus)..184

Quantum Identity Shifting: Becoming the Version of You Who Has Already Arrived...184

Chapter 15 (Bonus)..191

The Quantum Life Blueprint: Living as the Architect of Your Reality...191

Introduction

Awaken the Quantum Creator Within

What if the greatest breakthroughs in your life didn't require years of effort, but a shift in awareness?

What if the life you've dreamed of; greater freedom, abundance, health, love, and purpose, wasn't something you had to chase, but something you could tune into, like a frequency already vibrating within the quantum field?

This book is your invitation to step into that paradigm. To awaken to the truth that you are more than a collection of memories, routines, and roles. You are a conscious observer, a powerful architect of reality, participating in a dynamic, intelligent universe that responds to your thoughts, emotions, and intentions.

Bridging Ancient Wisdom and Quantum Science

For centuries, spiritual teachings have proclaimed the power of belief, attention, and intention. Now, quantum physics is catching up. Discoveries like the Observer Effect, wave-particle duality, superposition, and entanglement reveal that the fabric of reality is shaped not by fixed outcomes but by consciousness itself.

This book bridges the philosophical insights of the Law of Attraction and New Thought with the scientific breakthroughs of quantum mechanics. It offers a practical, step-by-step exploration of how your inner world creates your outer experience, and how to work with the universe as a conscious co-creator.

A Chapter-by-Chapter Journey of Transformation

Each chapter builds upon the last, offering not just knowledge but transformation:

- In **Chapter 1**, we begin with the foundation of the quantum mind and your power to direct thought.

- **Chapters 2 and 3** explore how duality and possibility shape your personal reality.

- In **Chapters 4 through 7**, you'll learn to harness observation, energy fields, interconnectedness, and uncertainty as allies in creation.

- **Chapters 8 through 10** guide you in manifesting desires, healing your body through consciousness, and achieving inner coherence.

- In **Chapter 11**, you'll bend time through intentional alignment with quantum timelines.

- **Chapter 12** teaches how to leap into new realities with bold, transformative action.

- **Chapter 13** invites you to explore the multiverse, where all possibilities already exist, and consciously choose among them.

- **Chapters 14 and 15**, our bonus chapters, go even deeper: one into the transformational power of identity, and the other into a complete 30-day quantum life blueprint for lasting integration.

From Knowing to Embodying

This is more than a book to read. It's a field to enter. A vibration to align with. Each concept is accompanied by stories, practices, and insights designed to shift your energy, expand your perception, and help you embody a new level of power and possibility.

You don't need to be a physicist to transform your life, you need only be willing to engage your awareness, tune your frequency, and act in alignment with the highest version of yourself.

Your Quantum Invitation

Whether you are just beginning your journey or have walked the path of self-mastery for years, this book meets you where you are and lifts you to where you are meant to be.

Welcome to your next level. Welcome to the edge of science and spirit. Welcome to your quantum life.

The universe is listening.

Now, let's begin.

How to Use This Book: Your Journey Through the Quantum Lens

This book is not just meant to be read, it's meant to be *experienced*.

Each chapter in this book is a gateway to a deeper understanding of your creative power and a practical invitation to embody it. While the insights are profound, they are not meant to remain intellectual, they are meant to reshape how you think, feel, act, and live.

Here's how to make the most of your journey:

1. Read Slowly, Reflect Deeply

This is not a novel to rush through, it's a manual for transformation. After each chapter, pause. Reflect on how the concepts relate to your life. Consider keeping a journal to capture your thoughts, shifts in awareness, and inspired actions.

2. Engage the Practices

Every chapter includes real-world examples, exercises, and questions to help you apply the principles. Don't skip them. They are designed to help you rewire your thoughts, align your emotions, and shift your energy. Transformation is in the doing.

3. Revisit Key Concepts

Quantum growth is layered. As you evolve, the same words will hit differently. Mark passages that move you, and return to them. You'll find new depth each time.

4. Use the Book as a Reference

After your first read, return to specific chapters as needed. If you're navigating uncertainty, revisit the chapter on the Uncertainty Principle. If you're preparing for a bold shift, jump to the Quantum Leap. Let this book become a lifelong companion in your evolution.

5. Create Your Quantum Practice

The final bonus chapter offers a 30-day blueprint to help you embody the entire book in daily life. Don't just finish the book, *integrate it.* Let it reshape how you live, love, lead, and dream.

6. Stay Open and Playful

Quantum transformation often unfolds in unexpected ways. Stay curious. Stay light. And trust that as you shift your inner world, the outer will reflect it.

Chapter 1

The Quantum Mind: Unlocking Your Thought Power

1. Introduction: The Mind as the Architect of Reality

Picture this: You wake up one morning with a deep sense that something in your life needs to change. Maybe it's your career, your relationships, or your financial situation. You've tried different approaches before, yet you find yourself stuck in the same patterns. But what if the key to transformation isn't in external action alone, but in how you **think and observe reality?**

Science is beginning to confirm what ancient wisdom has long suggested, **your thoughts are not just passive reflections of reality; they are active forces shaping it**. The world you experience is deeply influenced by the way you perceive it. Your beliefs, emotions, and mental focus act like a quantum lens, filtering and directing the energy around you.

At the heart of this concept lies the quantum mind, a principle suggesting that consciousness plays a fundamental role in how reality unfolds. In quantum physics, particles exist in multiple states until they are observed, at which point they take on a definite form. If this is true at the subatomic level, then what role does **your observation, focus, and belief** play in constructing your personal reality?

Throughout this chapter, we will explore the profound connection between quantum principles and **the power of the mind**. You will discover how your thoughts, emotions, and beliefs create patterns that shape your external world. Through real-life examples, scientific insights, and practical exercises, you will gain the tools to harness your mind's potential and begin transforming your life with intention.

1.1.   The Science Behind Thought Power

The Brain as a Quantum Processor

For decades, scientists believed that the brain functioned purely as a biochemical machine, reacting to stimuli in predictable ways. However, emerging research suggests that **the brain operates much like a quantum system**, processing vast amounts of information beyond linear cause-and-effect models.

Consider this: Every time you have a thought, **neural pathways** in your brain fire in response. These neural pathways are not fixed, they adapt, strengthen, or fade based on repetition and focus. This is the foundation of **neuroplasticity,** the brain's ability to rewire itself based on what you think about most often. In other words, what you repeatedly observe and focus on becomes reinforced in your mind, eventually manifesting in your external reality.

The Observer Effect and Conscious Creation

The Observer Effect, a cornerstone of quantum mechanics, suggests that **particles exist in multiple states until they are observed.** If this applies at the quantum level, then could your own awareness and focus **collapse possibilities into reality** in your life? This idea is more than just philosophical speculation, scientific studies in fields like psychology, neuroscience, and behavioral economics suggest that **what we expect and focus on influences what we perceive and experience.**

For example, studies on the **placebo effect** demonstrate how powerful belief is in shaping outcomes. When patients are given a sugar pill but are told it is a powerful drug, their bodies often respond **as if they have taken real medication**. This means that their **expectation alone** altered their physical state, a real-world manifestation of the mind's power over reality.

Practical Implications: Training Your Mind to Reshape Reality

If your mind can influence reality, the next question is: **How can you direct this power consciously?**

1. **Become Aware of Your Thoughts** – Throughout your day, take a moment to observe your mental patterns. Are your thoughts focused on what you want to create, or are they reinforcing limitations?

2. **Reframe Limiting Beliefs** – Identify recurring negative beliefs and replace them with empowering alternatives. Instead of "I'm not good at this," shift to "I am learning and improving every day."

3. **Use Visualization** – Spend a few minutes daily vividly imagining yourself achieving your goals. Neuroscientific research shows that the brain **responds to visualization as if it were real**, reinforcing positive outcomes.

4. **Direct Your Emotional Energy** – Your emotions fuel your thoughts. Cultivate **gratitude and excitement** to amplify the effects of your focus.

By mastering these mental techniques, you begin aligning your thoughts, emotions, and actions in a way that **reshapes your**

external reality. As we continue, we will delve deeper into how to refine this process and use it to consciously create the life you desire.

1.2.   The Mind-Reality Connection

How Thoughts Influence Your Perception

Imagine two individuals walking through the same city street, one sees opportunity, beauty, and potential, while the other notices only obstacles, chaos, and hardship. The street is the same, but their experiences are vastly different. Why? Because **perception is shaped by thought patterns**, and what you focus on determines how you interact with reality.

Your mind acts as a filter, processing an overwhelming amount of information and selecting what aligns with your **deepest beliefs and expectations**. In psychology, this is known as **selective attention**, you unconsciously tune in to what matches your internal state while filtering out the rest. If you constantly dwell on lack and limitation, you will notice more of it. Conversely, if you train your mind to focus on growth, abundance, and opportunity, your reality will begin to reflect those qualities.

The Self-Fulfilling Prophecy Effect

Your expectations shape your experiences. This concept, known as the **self-fulfilling prophecy**, suggests that what you anticipate, whether positive or negative, often becomes your reality. If you believe you are destined for success, you will subconsciously act in ways that align with that belief. If you believe you are bound to fail, your actions (or lack thereof) will reinforce that outcome.

A famous study in education demonstrated this effect: teachers were told that certain students (chosen at random) were academically gifted. As a result, those students received more encouragement and support, and by the end of the year, they **performed significantly better than their peers**. Their potential did not change, what changed was the belief system surrounding them, which influenced their outcomes.

This principle applies to every aspect of life: relationships, career, health, and personal success. Your **internal narrative dictates external results**. By consciously shifting your thoughts, you can begin directing reality toward the outcomes you desire.

1.3.   Breaking Free from Mental Limitations

The Power of Reprogramming Your Mind

Most people are not fully aware of the **mental programs** running their lives. These subconscious patterns, formed through past experiences, societal conditioning, and repetition, determine **what you believe is possible for you**. If you grew up hearing that money is scarce, that success requires struggle, or that you are not talented enough, these beliefs may still be shaping your reality, even if you consciously desire a different outcome.

The good news is that your brain is **not hardwired** to remain in these patterns forever. Thanks to **neuroplasticity**, you can reprogram your mind by intentionally changing your thought patterns. By consistently feeding your brain empowering beliefs, you **rewire** it to support success rather than limitation.

The Shift from Reaction to Creation

Most people go through life reacting to circumstances, believing that their environment dictates their emotions and actions. But true power comes from shifting from **reaction to creation**, from being at the mercy of external conditions to actively shaping them.

This shift happens when you:

1. **Identify Limiting Thoughts** – Pay close attention to repetitive thoughts that reinforce doubt, fear, or limitation.

2. **Challenge and Replace Them** – Whenever a limiting belief surfaces, question its validity and consciously replace it with an empowering alternative.

3. **Use Repetition and Emotion** – Your subconscious learns through repetition and emotion. Affirm your new beliefs daily with conviction and feeling.

4. **Take Aligned Action** – Thought alone is powerful, but action solidifies belief. Take steps that reinforce your new mindset.

By doing this, you shift from passively experiencing reality to **actively shaping it**. You become the architect of your life, using thought as the blueprint for the world you wish to create.

1.4.   Aligning Thought, Emotion, and Action

The Triad of Manifestation

Your thoughts are powerful, but they do not exist in isolation. To effectively shape reality, they must be **aligned with emotion and action**. This triad, **thought, emotion, and action**, creates the foundation for manifestation.

1. **Thought:** The blueprint, what you focus on and believe to be possible.

2. **Emotion:** The fuel, how deeply you feel and resonate with your thoughts.

3. **Action:** The bridge, the physical steps that bring your thoughts into reality.

When all three are in harmony, you enter a state of **coherence**, where your mental, emotional, and physical energies work together to materialize your desired outcomes. However, when one element is misaligned, such as thinking about success but feeling doubtful, or wanting change but taking no action, you create resistance that slows or blocks your progress.

The Role of Emotion in Reality Creation

Emotion is the **amplifier** of thought. Quantum physics suggests that energy responds to **frequency and vibration**, and your emotions generate a vibrational signal that interacts with the world around you. Positive emotions like gratitude, excitement, and love elevate your energy and attract circumstances that match that state. Conversely, negative emotions such as fear, doubt, or frustration lower your frequency and reinforce undesired outcomes.

This is why simply thinking about success is not enough. You must **feel** successful before tangible success appears. The process involves **embodying the emotional state** of your desired outcome in the present moment, rather than waiting for external validation.

Bridging Thought and Action

Many people fall into the trap of **passive wishing**, believing that thinking positively alone will bring change. However, the quantum mind operates most effectively when thought is accompanied by **intentional action**.

1. If you believe in abundance, act as though opportunities are already unfolding for you.

2. If you seek confidence, carry yourself as if you already possess it.

3. If you desire success, take steps, however small, that move you toward your goal.

Your actions send a powerful signal to both your subconscious mind and the external world, reinforcing your beliefs and accelerating your transformation.

1.5. Cultivating the Quantum Mindset

Shifting from Limitation to Possibility

The **quantum mindset** is about embracing **possibility over limitation**. Instead of seeing reality as rigid and fixed, you begin to view it as **fluid and responsive** to your consciousness. This shift allows you to:

1. **Move from scarcity to abundance** – Instead of seeing lack, you start recognizing the **infinite potential** available to you.

2. **Replace doubt with certainty** – Rather than questioning whether success is possible, you operate with the **assumption** that it is unfolding.

3. **Transform setbacks into opportunities** – Challenges become stepping stones rather than obstacles, helping you grow and refine your vision.

By adopting this mindset, you free yourself from the limitations of past experiences and step into a reality where **you are the creator, not just the observer**.

Daily Practices to Strengthen the Quantum Mind

1. **Morning Intention-Setting** – Begin each day by consciously choosing your dominant thoughts and emotions. Ask yourself, "What energy do I want to bring into today?"

2. **Mindful Awareness** – Regularly check in with your thoughts and emotions. If you catch yourself in a negative spiral, **pause, reset, and shift your focus**.

3. **Gratitude and Visualization** – Spend a few minutes each day feeling gratitude for what you have and visualizing your desired reality **as if it already exists**.

4. **Take Inspired Action** – Make decisions and take actions that align with your vision. Even small steps create momentum.

The quantum mind is not about wishful thinking, it is about **intentionally aligning your thoughts, emotions, and actions to shape your reality**. The more you strengthen this mindset, the more fluid and limitless your world becomes.

1.6. Reprogramming Your Mind for Quantum Change

The Subconscious: The Gateway to Transformation

While conscious thought plays a key role in shaping reality, **your subconscious mind** is the deeper force that governs your long-term beliefs, habits, and automatic responses. Think of your subconscious as the operating system running in the background, it influences your perceptions, decisions, and behaviors without you even realizing it.

Scientific research shows that **up to 95% of your daily actions are driven by subconscious programming**. If this programming is filled with limiting beliefs, doubts, or negative expectations, it will override your conscious desires for success, happiness, and abundance.

The good news? **You can reprogram your subconscious mind** just as you would update outdated software.

Techniques for Reprogramming the Mind

1. **Affirmations with Emotional Charge**

Repeating affirmations is not enough, you must **feel** them as deeply as possible. Instead of mechanically saying, "I am successful," close your eyes, visualize success vividly, and embody the emotions that come with it.

2. **Meditation and Mental Rehearsal**

Meditation quiets the analytical mind, allowing direct access to the subconscious. In this relaxed state, you can **impress new beliefs and mental images** that reshape your reality.

Mental rehearsal, used by elite athletes and peak performers, creates **neural pathways** that make success feel familiar before it physically manifests.

3. **Pattern Disruption**

If you catch yourself engaging in negative thought loops, interrupt them. Stand up, move, or use a **pattern-breaking phrase** like "Cancel! Replace!" and immediately focus on a positive alternative.

4. **Immersion in New Environments**

Surround yourself with people, books, and experiences that reflect the reality you want to create. Your mind adapts to the dominant energy in your environment.

By consistently applying these techniques, you **override old programming** and align your subconscious with the quantum principles of conscious creation.

Conclusion: Becoming the Architect of Your Reality

At its core, the **quantum mind** is not just a theory, it is a way of being. It is the understanding that **your thoughts, emotions, and actions are not passive but active forces shaping your reality**. Science and philosophy converge on this truth: **What you focus on, you become. What you expect, you attract. What you believe, you create.**

The Key Takeaways from This Chapter

1. Your **consciousness influences reality**, just as the observer influences quantum particles.

2. Your mind operates like a **quantum processor**, shaping your experiences based on focus and belief.

3. Thought alone is not enough, **emotion and action** must be aligned to manifest results.

4. The subconscious mind is the **gatekeeper of transformation**, reprogramming it allows for radical change.

As you move forward in this book, you will continue uncovering deeper insights into how quantum principles apply to **your thoughts, decisions, and very existence**. The next chapter, **Wave-Particle Duality, Balancing Potential and Action**, will build upon this foundation, guiding you through the fascinating interplay between potential and action. By understanding the principles of wave-particle duality, you'll learn how to harness your innate potential and transform it into purposeful actions, achieving a harmonious balance in your personal and professional life.

Your mind is your most powerful tool, use it wisely, and reality will bend in your favor.

Chapter 2

Wave-Particle Duality: Balancing Potential and Action

2. Introduction: The Dance Between Possibility and Manifestation

Imagine standing at the edge of a vast ocean, watching the waves ripple across the surface. Beneath those waves lies an unseen depth, a realm of stillness and infinite potential. In much the same way, your life oscillates between two fundamental states: the realm of possibility and the realm of action. This dynamic balance is at the heart of **wave-particle duality**, a principle in quantum mechanics that reveals how matter can exist as both a wave (potential) and a particle (manifested reality), depending on observation and interaction.

Your dreams, goals, and aspirations first exist in a wave-like state, fluid, unformed, full of infinite potential. The moment you take decisive action, you collapse those possibilities into a defined reality, much like a particle taking on a solid form. However, the challenge many face is either remaining stuck in endless possibility without taking action or becoming too rigid in action without allowing for new possibilities to emerge.

In this chapter, we explore how understanding and applying the principle of wave-particle duality can help you find the **balance between potential and action**, between dreaming and doing. Mastering this balance is the key to unlocking your ability to consciously shape your life with both clarity and fluidity.

2.1.   The Science Behind Wave-Particle Duality

A Paradox of Nature

Wave-particle duality is one of the most intriguing concepts in quantum physics. It suggests that particles, such as electrons and photons, can behave as both waves and particles. Their nature is not fixed but depends on how they are observed. This was famously demonstrated in the **double-slit experiment**, where light and electrons exhibited wave-like behavior when unobserved but transformed into distinct particles when measured.

This paradox challenges the traditional view of reality as something fixed and independent of observation. Instead, it suggests that **existence is fluid and shaped by interaction**, meaning that potential and manifestation are intertwined in ways we are only beginning to understand.

The Human Parallel: Living as Both Wave and Particle

If matter at its most fundamental level can exist in two states, what does this mean for you? Just as light can be a wave or a particle, your reality exists in two forms:

1. **Wave State (Potential)** – Your dreams, ideas, and possibilities before they take shape. This is the realm of imagination, intuition, and intention.

2. **Particle State (Manifestation)** – The tangible results of your actions and decisions. This is where ideas solidify into reality through effort and commitment.

Success in life requires mastering the **fluid transition between these two states**, knowing when to explore possibility and when to commit to action.

2.2. The Trap of Infinite Potential: When Waves Never Collapse

Many people remain trapped in the **wave-like state of endless possibility**, dreaming, planning, and visualizing their ideal lives but never taking the necessary steps to manifest them. They live in a world of potential energy that never converts into tangible reality. Just like a quantum wave that remains uncollapsed, their aspirations remain suspended in the realm of possibility, never materializing into action.

This often happens due to:

1. **Fear of failure** – Worrying that taking action might lead to rejection, disappointment, or mistakes.

2. **Perfectionism** – Feeling the need to have every detail figured out before making a move.

3. **Overthinking** – Analyzing and weighing options indefinitely without making a firm decision.

4. **Attachment to multiple possibilities** – Fearing that committing to one choice will mean sacrificing other potential opportunities.

This state of **analysis paralysis** keeps you stuck in perpetual inaction, much like a wave that never crashes onto shore. The truth is, possibility alone is not enough, **you must collapse the wave into reality through action**.

Breaking Free: Shifting from Potential to Action

To escape this trap and move from mere potential to tangible progress, you must **embrace decision-making and take inspired action**. Here's how:

1. **Set a Clear Intention** – Clearly define what you want to create. The more precise your vision, the easier it is to manifest.

2. **Take an Immediate Step** – The moment you take even the smallest action, you initiate the process of reality formation.

3. **Embrace Imperfection** – Perfection is an illusion; progress comes from learning through action. Start now, refine later.

4. **Limit Overthinking** – Set a deadline for decisions. Overanalyzing kills momentum.

5. **Trust the Process** – Clarity often comes through action, not before it. Have faith that things will unfold as they should.

By consciously collapsing the wave through intentional action, you move from being a **passive dreamer** to an **active creator** of your life.

2.3. The Rigidity of Overcommitment: When Particles Lose Fluidity

While some people remain trapped in infinite potential, others swing too far in the opposite direction, locking themselves into rigid action, **treating themselves as fixed particles with no room for change**.

This rigidity manifests as:

1. **A fixed mindset** – Believing that success must come in one specific way and resisting alternative paths.

2. **Resistance to change** – Ignoring signs that a new approach may be necessary.

3. **Forcing outcomes** – Pushing relentlessly toward a goal, even when intuition suggests a course correction.

This is like a quantum particle that has collapsed into one definite state, losing its adaptability and openness to new possibilities. **Overcommitment to a single course of action can lead to burnout, frustration, and stagnation.**

Cultivating Flexibility: Balancing Action with Adaptability

To maintain progress while allowing room for growth and change, practice **flexible persistence**:

1. **Stay Open to Adjustments** – Be committed to your goal but flexible about how it manifests.

2. **Pay Attention to Feedback** – Life constantly provides clues, listen to them and adjust your approach.

3. **Adopt a Growth Mindset** – See setbacks as opportunities to learn and refine your strategy.

4. **Make Room for Flow** – Sometimes the best results come when you ease up and allow synchronicity to work in your favor.

By integrating both **wave-like openness and particle-like decisiveness**, you create a life where **intention and action work in harmony**, allowing you to manifest your highest vision **without rigidity or hesitation**.

2.4. Mastering the Dance: Integrating Potential and Action

True success in life comes from learning to **consciously shift between the wave and particle states**, knowing when to explore possibilities and when to take decisive action. Just as quantum particles naturally oscillate between these two states, you must cultivate the ability to move fluidly between **imagination and execution**.

The key is to recognize that neither state is inherently superior, **both are necessary** for creating a fulfilling and dynamic life.

1. If you only dwell in the wave state of infinite possibilities, you **risk never bringing your dreams to life**.

2. If you only exist in the particle state of rigid action, you **risk limiting yourself to a single path and missing new opportunities**.

The **most effective creators, innovators, and leaders know how to transition between these states effortlessly,** leveraging the power of possibility while also committing to action.

Strategies for Balancing Potential and Action

To cultivate this mastery, practice the following:

1. **Align with Your Core Vision** – Keep your bigger purpose in mind. This allows you to explore possibilities without losing direction.

2. **Use Periods of Reflection** – Set aside time for deep thought, creative brainstorming, and strategic planning before jumping into action.

3. **Adopt a Bias Toward Action** – When faced with hesitation, take small steps forward. Action leads to momentum.

4. **Remain Open to Adjustments** – Take action boldly, but be willing to refine your approach as new information emerges.

5. **Trust Intuition and Synchronicity** – Not every move needs to be logically planned. Some of the best breakthroughs come from following inspired instincts.

By mastering this **dance between potential and action,** you unlock the ability to **shape reality with both creativity and decisiveness**.

2.5. The Quantum Creator: Consciously Shaping Your Reality

The principles of wave-particle duality reveal a profound truth: **you are not merely a passive observer of life, you are an active participant in its creation.** Just as quantum particles respond to observation, your reality responds to your **intentions, focus, and actions.**

You are not bound by a single, fixed path. **You have the power to shape your existence by consciously choosing when to dream and when to act.**

The Power of Awareness

To fully step into your role as a conscious creator, cultivate **self-awareness** in the following ways:

1. **Notice when you're stuck in endless possibilities** – If you find yourself endlessly planning without acting, push yourself to take the first step.

2. **Notice when you're too rigid in your actions** – If you're forcing results without flow, take a step back to explore new possibilities.

3. **Regularly recalibrate your approach** – Just as quantum particles remain in motion, so should your life be a dynamic process of refinement and growth.

Living in Quantum Alignment

To align with the quantum model of reality, practice the **art of fluid creation:**

1. **Set clear yet flexible intentions** – Be specific about your desires but allow space for the universe to deliver in unexpected ways.

2. **Move forward with inspired action** – Take steps in alignment with your vision, but stay adaptable.

3. **Trust the timing of manifestation** – Some dreams take time to materialize. Patience and persistence create momentum.

4. **Embrace uncertainty as a creative force** – The unknown is where possibilities exist. Rather than fearing it, learn to navigate it with confidence.

By mastering wave-particle duality in your life, you transform from a passive reactor to an **intentional architect of your reality**.

This understanding naturally leads to the next great quantum concept: **Superposition, the realization that you are never limited to just one possibility at any given moment.**

2.6.   The Flow State: The Sweet Spot Between Possibility and Action

When you master the ability to shift between wave-like potential and particle-like action, you unlock what many call **"the flow state."** This is the mental state where you are completely immersed in an activity, fully present, highly focused, and effortlessly effective.

In quantum terms, flow is the **perfect equilibrium between wave and particle states**, where creativity (wave) and execution (particle) merge seamlessly. Athletes describe it as "being in the zone," artists call it "creative inspiration," and scientists experience it as moments of sudden breakthrough.

The Science of Flow

Psychologists have studied the flow state extensively, identifying several key characteristics:

1. **Complete focus and absorption in the task** – Time seems to disappear, and distractions fade.

2. **A balance between challenge and skill** – The task is engaging but not overwhelming.

3. **Effortless action and immediate feedback** – Every move feels natural and well-timed.

4. **Loss of self-consciousness** – Doubt and overthinking vanish, replaced by full presence.

From a quantum perspective, flow happens when you stop resisting and align your actions with your inner vision, allowing energy to move freely between **potential and manifestation.**

Cultivating Flow in Your Daily Life

To enter the flow state more often, practice the following:

1. **Set Clear, Meaningful Goals** – Define what you want to achieve in a way that excites and motivates you.

2. **Eliminate Distractions** – Create an environment that minimizes interruptions and fosters deep concentration.

3. **Engage in Activities That Challenge and Excite You** – Flow emerges when your skills are stretched just beyond their current limit.

4. **Trust the Process and Let Go of Overthinking** – The more you try to force flow, the more elusive it becomes. Surrender to the moment.

5. **Prioritize Rest and Recovery** – Flow is easier to access when your mind and body are well-rested.

By mastering the flow state, you **effortlessly harmonize between possibility and action**, making success feel natural rather than forced.

Conclusion: Becoming the Quantum Architect of Your Life

Wave-particle duality is more than just a principle of quantum physics, it is a **blueprint for mastering life itself.** By understanding when to embrace the **fluidity of possibility** and when to commit to **decisive action**, you become the conscious creator of your reality.

Key Takeaways

1. **Your reality exists in two states:** the **wave of infinite possibilities** and the **particle of manifested action.**

2. **Being stuck in pure possibility leads to inaction, while rigid action limits growth.** Mastering both states creates balance.

3. The most successful individuals flow between these two states, knowing when to dream and when to act.

4. By accessing the flow state, you unlock effortless momentum, where clarity, creativity, and execution merge.

Moving Forward

Now that you understand the power of **balancing potential and action**, the next step is to **expand your perception of what is possible**.

In the next chapter, we dive into the concept of **Superposition,** the realization that at any given moment, you are not confined to just one reality. Instead, infinite possibilities exist simultaneously, waiting for you to choose and collapse them into being.

Chapter 3

Superposition: The Infinite Possibilities of Being

3. Introduction: Unlocking Infinite Potential

Every decision you make, every path you take, is just one of countless possibilities available to you at any given moment. Imagine standing at a crossroads with infinite roads extending in all directions, each road represents a version of your life that could unfold based on your choices. This is the essence of **superposition**, a concept from quantum physics that reveals how all possible states exist simultaneously until one is observed and chosen.

But what if the only thing keeping you from stepping into your highest potential is the belief that you are limited? What if, instead of seeing obstacles, you saw endless opportunities waiting to be chosen?

In this chapter, we explore how **superposition applies to human potential**. You are not bound to a singular path. Instead, you exist in a field of **limitless possibilities**, where your thoughts, beliefs, and choices determine the reality you step into. **The key to success is learning to collapse the quantum wave into the version of reality that aligns with your highest desires.**

By understanding and applying this principle, you can **break free from limiting patterns** and consciously create a future that excites and empowers you. Let's dive in.

3.1.   The Quantum Superposition of You: A Universe of Possibilities

In the world of quantum mechanics, a single particle can exist in multiple states at the same time. It remains in this **superposition** until it is observed, at which point it "collapses" into a definite state. The fascinating part? **The same principle applies to you.**

At this very moment, your life exists in multiple potential states. There is a version of you that is wealthy, successful, and fulfilled. There is also a version struggling with limitations and doubts. Both exist as **possibilities in the quantum field,** and the version that manifests is the one you consciously (or unconsciously) observe and focus on.

This means you are far more powerful than you may realize. Every time you make a decision, big or small, you are choosing which version of yourself you step into.

Breaking Free from the Illusion of Limitation

Most people live as if they are stuck in a pre-determined reality. They assume that their circumstances, past experiences, or external limitations define their future. But quantum physics tells us otherwise. **Reality is fluid, not fixed.**

Think of yourself as a **quantum being**, always in flux, always containing multiple potential outcomes. If you see yourself as limited, you collapse into that limitation. But the moment you **believe in a new possibility**, the quantum field reorganizes to match that belief.

To **thrive in a state of infinite potential**, you must:

1.   **Become aware of your choices**: Every decision you make shifts you toward one version of reality or another. Are your daily choices aligning with the future you desire?

2. **Expand your self-concept**: Instead of seeing yourself as "stuck" in a single version of life, recognize that multiple futures exist, waiting for you to claim them.

3. **Deliberately choose empowering thoughts and beliefs**: Your attention is the observer that determines which potential becomes real. Focus on possibilities rather than limitations.

3.2. The Observer Effect: The Power of Your Focus

At the heart of quantum physics lies a profound mystery: **the observer effect**. Scientists have found that when they observe a particle, it behaves differently than when it is unobserved. In other words, the mere act of observation influences reality.

What does this mean for you? **Your focus, what you consistently observe and give attention to, shapes your reality.**

If you constantly focus on lack, struggle, and limitations, your reality collapses into that state. If you shift your attention to possibility, abundance, and success, the quantum field adjusts accordingly. **You are not just a passive participant in life; you are the observer shaping your personal universe.**

How to Apply the Observer Effect in Your Life

Your life follows the same quantum principle: **where your attention goes, energy flows, and reality follows.** To harness this power, you must become intentional about what you observe and focus on.

1. **Choose the Reality You Want to Observe**
   Every moment presents multiple potential outcomes. Will you focus on the version of yourself that is struggling, or the one that is thriving? Intentionally **observe** the reality you wish to experience.

2. **Shift Your Inner Narrative**
   Your dominant thoughts act as the observer that collapses your reality. If your mental script is filled with doubt and fear, your life will reflect that. Reprogram your mind with empowering beliefs that align with the future you desire.

3. **Practice Visualization and Affirmation**
   Visualization is a powerful tool that allows you to pre-select your reality. Athletes, performers, and high achievers use it to mentally rehearse success before it happens. Spend time each day **seeing and feeling** yourself in your desired reality.

Try This: The Quantum Focus Exercise

For the next 7 days, practice **conscious observation**:

1. Identify an area of life you want to shift (wealth, health, relationships, etc.).

2. Observe your current thoughts about this area, are they positive or limiting?

3. Intentionally shift your focus toward the best possible outcome.

4. Each day, visualize yourself already experiencing that desired reality.

Observe how your mindset, and eventually your external reality, begins to shift.

3.3.   The Collapse of Possibility: Why People Get Stuck

If infinite possibilities exist, why do so many people feel trapped in repetitive cycles of struggle? The answer lies in **unconscious observation.**

Most people unknowingly collapse their reality into the same patterns by focusing on the **past** or reinforcing limiting beliefs. They observe their struggles, replay past failures, and expect more of the same, unintentionally locking themselves into that version of reality.

Every day, you are making an observation, whether consciously or unconsciously, that determines the reality you step into. If you observe life through the lens of doubt, lack, or fear, the quantum field responds in kind, collapsing into experiences that confirm those expectations.

Breaking Free from Repetitive Patterns

To create new outcomes, you must stop unconsciously collapsing into old limitations. Here's how:

1.   **Detach   from   the   Past**
      The past only exists if you keep observing it. If you constantly reference past failures, you keep reinforcing them. Instead, shift your attention to new possibilities.

2.   **Question   Your   Limiting   Beliefs**
      Many limitations are not real, they are inherited

thoughts you have accepted as truth. Challenge these beliefs and replace them with new empowering ones.

3. **Live in the Energy of the Future You Want**
Your emotions are powerful signals to the quantum field. Instead of waiting for external proof, feel the emotions of your desired reality **now**.

Try This: The Reality Reset Exercise

1. **Identify a Repetitive Struggle** – Is there a recurring challenge in your life? Money problems? Relationship issues? Self-doubt?

2. **Observe Your Current Focus** – What thoughts, beliefs, and emotions are reinforcing this pattern?

3. **Shift Your Observation** – Stop feeding attention to the struggle. Instead, visualize a new outcome daily.

4. **Feel the Shift** – Step into the version of yourself that has already moved past this struggle. Act as if this reality is unfolding now.

When you stop focusing on limitations and start **observing potential**, you initiate a quantum shift in your life.

3.4. Becoming the Architect of Your Reality

Once you understand that your attention determines your reality, you gain the power to **consciously design your life.** Instead of reacting to circumstances, you become the deliberate creator of your experiences.

The key is to apply **intentional observation**, aligning your thoughts, emotions, and actions with the reality you want to experience. Just as a scientist sets up an experiment to yield a specific result, you must set up your mind and energy to attract your desired reality.

The Three Pillars of Conscious Creation

1. **Clarity** – Define the reality you want to observe. Vagueness leads to mixed results. The clearer you are about your desires, the easier it is to manifest them.
2. **Emotional Alignment** – Your emotions act as signals to the quantum field. Instead of waiting for external proof, embody the feelings of success, joy, and abundance now.
3. **Inspired Action** – Observation alone isn't enough. You must take aligned action toward your desired outcome, reinforcing your belief in its reality.

Try This: The Future Self Experiment

For the next 7 days, practice living as if your desired future is already unfolding:

1. **Visualize Your Ideal Reality** – Spend 5 minutes daily seeing yourself in the reality you want.

2. **Feel the Emotions of That Reality** – Embody confidence, excitement, and gratitude as if it's already happening.

3. **Take One Small Aligned Action** – Each day, do something that affirms this future version of you.

As you commit to this practice, you'll notice a shift, opportunities aligning, synchronicities appearing, and doors opening where there were none before.

Key Takeaway: You Are the Observer and the Creator

The reality you experience is the one you observe most often. If you want to change your life, start by **changing what you focus on.**

In the next section, we'll explore how to maintain this quantum awareness in daily life and ensure you stay aligned with your highest potential.

3.5. Sustaining Quantum Awareness in Everyday Life

Understanding that your focus determines reality is one thing, **living it daily** is another. The challenge most people face is that they gain moments of clarity but quickly fall back into old thought patterns.

To **sustain** quantum awareness and consistently align with your highest potential, you must train yourself to observe reality with **intention** rather than react unconsciously.

The Power of Daily Observation

Your current reality is a reflection of what you observe most often. If you spend the majority of your time focusing on stress, limitations, or lack, those patterns persist. However, if you shift your observation toward abundance, possibility, and success, you begin collapsing those realities instead.

The key is to create a **daily practice** that keeps you aligned with the version of reality you desire.

Quantum Awareness Practices

Here are powerful ways to maintain **intentional observation** and stay in alignment with your highest reality:

The 3-Minute Morning Reset

Each morning, before checking your phone or engaging with the outside world, spend three minutes doing the following:

1. **Set Your Observation Point** – Decide what kind of day you want to experience. Instead of waiting to see what happens, declare how you want to feel and what you want to attract.
2. **Feel It Before It Happens** – Close your eyes and embody the emotions of the version of yourself already thriving.
3. **Affirm Your Quantum Identity** – Say: *I am the creator of my reality. Today, I choose to observe and align with abundance, joy, and success.*

This practice ensures that you **start each day in alignment**, consciously directing your focus rather than being pulled into external distractions.

The Awareness Check-In

Throughout the day, pause and ask yourself:

1. *What am I focusing on right now?*

2. *Is this focus aligning with the reality I want to create?*

3. *What thought shift can I make in this moment?*

These quick check-ins **interrupt autopilot thinking** and allow you to realign with your intentions.

The Nightly Quantum Reflection

Before bed, reflect on your day with **intentional gratitude**:

1. **Acknowledge Your Wins** – What evidence of alignment did you notice today? Did an opportunity show up? Did you feel more empowered? Recognizing these moments strengthens your belief in quantum alignment.

2. **Release Resistance** – If you found yourself stuck in old patterns, don't dwell on them. Instead, simply acknowledge them and **choose to shift tomorrow.**

3. **Visualize Tomorrow's Reality** – Close your eyes and see yourself already thriving in the next 24 hours. This imprints the quantum field with the reality you desire.

Living as the Conscious Creator

By integrating these daily awareness practices, you ensure that you **consistently observe and collapse realities** that align with your highest potential.

Key Insight: *The more you reinforce a new reality, the faster it solidifies as your experience.*

3.6.   The Observer Effect: Choosing Your Reality

The Observer Effect in quantum mechanics reveals that the mere act of observation influences the behavior of particles. This principle carries profound implications for personal transformation, it suggests that where you place your attention determines what manifests in your reality.

Your thoughts act as the lens through which you observe the quantum field. If your focus is on lack, struggle, or fear, your reality will reflect those frequencies. But if you train yourself to observe possibility, abundance, and success, you shift into a reality where these elements become tangible.

Directing Your Conscious Observation

1. **Become Aware of Your Mental Lens** – Notice what thoughts dominate your mind. Are you seeing opportunities or limitations? The first step in shifting reality is shifting perception.

2. **Reframe Your Inner Narrative** – Every moment presents a choice: do you observe failure, or do you observe growth? Train yourself to reframe challenges as stepping stones rather than obstacles.

3. **Hold the Vision with Conviction** – Just as a scientist's measurement determines a particle's state, your consistent attention solidifies potential outcomes into reality. What you expect is what you attract.

Try this: **Conscious Observation Practice**

1. Each morning, set an intention to observe only possibilities aligned with your highest aspirations.

2. When challenges arise, pause and reframe them as opportunities.

3. At night, reflect on moments where your conscious observation influenced a positive shift.

The more intentional you are with your focus, the more powerful your ability to shape reality.

Conclusion: You Are the Superposition

You are not limited to the path you've walked or the thoughts you've previously entertained. Within you exists a vast array of possibilities, parallel versions of yourself waiting for your conscious attention to bring them to life. Just like the electron in superposition, you can hold space for multiple realities until you choose to collapse one into existence.

The practice of creative visualization is not about daydreaming or fantasy, it is a tool of quantum alignment. When you imagine with clarity and emotion, you step into resonance with the reality you desire. Your brain begins to rewire, your emotions shift to match the frequency of that vision, and your actions begin to align.

You are both the observer and the creator. When you visualize, you are rehearsing the future. When you feel it as real, you're shaping your energetic signature to call it into being.

Let this chapter be your reminder that you don't need to "wait" for your dreams to come true. You can live from them now. You can hold the vibration, embody the state, and act in alignment with the version of you who has already arrived.

Final Reflection: What vision have you been holding at arm's length, waiting for permission to believe in?

Stop waiting.

The quantum field is listening.

Visualize it!

Feel it.

Collapse the wave into your new reality.

In the next chapter, we'll explore how mindful observation further enhances your manifestation power, revealing how The Observer Effect shapes the unfolding of your life moment by moment.

Chapter 4

The Observer Effect: Mindfulness for Success

4. Introduction: The Power of Observation

Imagine a talented musician stepping onto a brightly lit stage, heart pounding, mind swirling with doubt and anxiety. In that critical moment, she pauses, closes her eyes, and consciously observes her thoughts and emotions without judgment. As she breathes deeply, anxiety shifts into clarity. Her performance is flawless, captivating everyone in the room. This transformation illustrates the profound power of mindful observation, the real-world embodiment of the Observer Effect.

The Observer Effect, initially discovered in quantum physics, reveals that the mere act of observing a particle affects its state. Similarly, your focused attention shapes the experiences unfolding in your life. Every day, you subconsciously filter reality through beliefs, emotions, and expectations, influencing your outcomes more profoundly than you might realize.

Think of your mind as a spotlight: wherever you direct your awareness, you illuminate possibilities. The life you live today reflects the areas you've chosen, consciously or unconsciously, to observe most. Your relationships, career, health, and wealth all mirror the attention you've given them.

But there's a deeper truth many overlook: observation alone isn't enough. Just like in quantum experiments, where intention and interaction affect outcomes, your focus must be energized with clear purpose and aligned action. Passive manifestation, merely hoping or visualizing, isn't what creates lasting change. Quantum reality responds to coherent intention and vibrational alignment.

In this chapter, you will master the art of mindful observation fused with conscious intention. You'll discover how shifting your awareness deliberately, and backing it with aligned emotion and action, can transform your life, manifesting success, wealth, and fulfillment. By becoming a deliberate observer and an empowered creator, you actively shape your reality, turning potential into tangible outcomes.

4.1.   Observers as Reality Shapers

The Observer Effect was famously demonstrated by the Double-Slit Experiment in quantum physics, where particles changed their behavior based solely on observation. Without observation, particles exist in multiple states simultaneously, known as quantum superposition. However, when observed, these possibilities collapse into a single, tangible reality.

Your life follows a similar principle. Until you consciously observe your potential, your dreams remain suspended in possibility. But the moment you direct intentional, mindful attention toward your goals, and match it with belief and inspired action, you collapse these possibilities into concrete realities.

Consider Nikola Tesla, a visionary inventor renowned for his groundbreaking work on electricity and wireless communication. Tesla famously emphasized, "If you want to find the secrets of the universe, think in terms of energy, frequency, and vibration." Tesla intuitively understood the Observer Effect long before it became widely known in quantum physics. By consciously tuning into specific outcomes and working from inspired ideas, he repeatedly manifested innovations that changed the world.

Similarly, when you become aware of your subconscious beliefs and emotional states, you gain power over the reality you experience. Mindful observation allows you to deliberately choose what you focus on, influence outcomes, and then act from that awareness.

But intention is the missing link in many manifestation teachings. Intention is focused energy, it is observation with purpose. When paired with consistent inspired action, it signals the quantum field with clarity and strength, drawing the corresponding reality into your experience.

Passive wishing is observation without energy. Quantum intention is observation infused with power, purpose, and motion.

Take a moment now and reflect: What outcomes have you unconsciously created through passive observation? What realities could you consciously manifest by directing powerful, purposeful attention toward them, and acting accordingly?

The sections ahead will guide you step-by-step in harnessing the Observer Effect as an intentional and empowered creator, allowing you to shape your reality with awareness, energy, and conscious choice.

4.2.   Mindfulness: Harnessing the Power of the Present Moment

Mindfulness is the practice of intentionally paying attention to the present moment without judgment. It sharpens your ability to consciously direct your awareness and is the foundation of empowered observation.

Imagine standing at the edge of a river, watching the water flow by. Your thoughts and emotions pass like currents, but mindfulness allows you to observe them without getting swept away. You become the calm presence behind the stream of thoughts.

Take Jon Kabat-Zinn, the founder of the Mindfulness-Based Stress Reduction (MBSR) program. He has helped countless individuals manage stress, anxiety, and chronic pain through mindfulness practices. By observing his mental patterns rather than reacting to them, he demonstrated how mindfulness can transform one's approach to life's challenges. Instead of spiraling into overthinking, he paused, grounded himself, and redirected his focus to empowering possibilities. Over time, this simple shift gave him clarity, emotional control, and renewed confidence.

Steps to Integrate Mindfulness:

1. **Daily Meditation**: Dedicate at least 10 minutes each day to stillness. Sit comfortably, observe your breath, and watch your thoughts arise and pass without attachment.

2. **Present-Moment Awareness**: Throughout your day, pause and check in with your senses. What do you see, hear, feel, or smell right now? Ground yourself in the now.

3. **Intentional Redirection**: When you catch yourself dwelling on limiting thoughts, gently bring your awareness back to a chosen intention or affirmation.

Mindfulness creates space between stimulus and response. It allows you to shift from autopilot into conscious creation, aligning your attention and energy with your highest goals.

4.3.   Observing with Intention: The Missing Ingredient in Manifestation

Many people believe manifestation is about visualizing and waiting for the universe to deliver. But manifestation without intention is like observing without engaging, it lacks direction and power.

The quantum field doesn't respond to hope; it responds to resonance. It mirrors your dominant energetic signal. That signal is shaped by how you observe yourself, your desires, and your world, with energy, belief, and action.

True manifestation begins when you shift from passive daydreaming to active co-creation.

The Three Pillars of Quantum Intention:

1.   **Clarity of Desire**: Know what you want and why. Vague desires produce vague results. Specificity focuses your observation.

2.   **Emotional Embodiment**: Feel the reality of your desire now. Emotions are the energetic fuel that makes your intention magnetic.

3.   **Aligned Action**: Every observation must be followed by congruent steps. Action confirms belief and anchors new realities.

Mindful observation, infused with clarity, emotion, and action, transforms your role from passive observer to conscious architect of your life.

"Intent is not a hope. It's a declaration.", James Cameron, multiple Academy Awards winner.

In the next sections, we'll explore how your inner dialogue reinforces your observations, and how to master it to sustain your shift into empowered co-creation.

4.4. Mindfulness in Action: Practical Techniques for Daily Life

Mindfulness is not just about stillness, it's about showing up to life with full awareness and intention. When practiced daily, mindfulness becomes a gateway to aligning your inner world with your outer success. It empowers you to direct your focus consciously, choosing your thoughts, emotions, and actions in alignment with your goals.

Picture yourself as a skilled gardener. Every thought you think, every emotion you feel, and every action you take is a seed. Mindfulness is your ability to plant those seeds with care and to pull out the weeds of unconscious reactivity.

Daily Mindfulness Practices for Empowered Living:

1. **Morning Mindful Intention**

    Upon waking, sit for a few quiet minutes. Ask yourself: "What energy do I want to embody today?" Choose a clear intention, calm, courage, joy, and let it guide your awareness.

2. **Observation Breaks**

    Set reminders to pause during the day. Take 1-2 minutes to observe your thoughts and emotions. Are you aligned with your intention? If not, gently realign.

3. **Mindful Decision-Making**

    Before making a choice, pause and observe: "Am I acting from fear or clarity?" This moment of mindfulness can redirect your path toward greater alignment.

4. **Gratitude Moments**

    Several times a day, intentionally observe something you're grateful for. Gratitude is a powerful frequency that shifts your observation from lack to abundance.

5. **Evening Reflection Journal**

    Reflect on your day. What did you observe most? How did mindfulness shift your outcomes? This practice deepens awareness and strengthens your conscious creation muscles.

These techniques train your mind to focus with precision. The more mindful you are, the more powerfully you engage the Observer Effect to shape reality intentionally.

4.5.   Observer Mastery: A 7-Day Mindfulness Challenge

To truly integrate the Observer Effect, consistency is key. This 7-Day Mindfulness Challenge will help you cultivate powerful awareness, reset your focus, and begin manifesting with intention.

Day 1: Awareness Reset

Activity: Observe your dominant thoughts. Write down the top 5 recurring ones.

Reflection: Are these thoughts aligned with the life you desire?

Day 2: Morning Intention + Evening Reflection

Activity: Set a clear intention in the morning. Reflect at night on how it shaped your day.

Reflection: What showed up differently when you held your intention in focus?

Day 3: Reframe the Narrative

Activity: Catch a limiting thought and reframe it in the moment.

Reflection: How did this shift change your emotional state and behavior?

Day 4: Emotional Anchoring

Activity: When a powerful emotion arises (joy, peace, confidence), anchor it with a deep breath and a physical gesture (like touching your heart).

Reflection: How did you use that anchor later to reset your state?

Day 5: Observer Pause

Activity: Before reacting, pause. Observe your internal response.

Reflection: Did this pause lead to a more empowered response?

Day 6: Visualization with Intention

Activity: Spend 10 minutes visualizing a goal. Feel it, embody it, observe it as done.

Reflection: What did you notice about your thoughts and feelings during and after?

Day 7: Integration and Choice

Activity: Reflect on your week. What shifted? What practices felt most powerful?

Reflection: What will you continue integrating into your daily life?

By the end of this challenge, you will have built a mindfulness habit that activates the Observer Effect at will, helping you live more consciously, confidently, and creatively.

4.6.   Mindful Observation in Action: Manifesting Through Daily Awareness

Mindfulness is not just a practice, it's a way of being. When paired with the Observer Effect, mindfulness becomes a daily tool for creation, aligning your inner state with your desired outer reality. The more consistently you observe with intention, the more the quantum field reflects your focused awareness back to you in the form of experiences, opportunities, and synchronicities.

Practical Strategies for Mindful Manifestation:

1. **Daily Intention Setting**: Each morning, define what you wish to experience or embody. Anchor that intention with a powerful affirmation.

2. **Observer Check-Ins**: Set alarms to pause and ask, "What am I observing right now? Does it align with what I want to create?"

3. **Conscious Language**: Speak as though your desires are unfolding now. Words direct energy.

4. **Gratitude Observation**: At the end of your day, journal about what went well. Acknowledge how your focus influenced your outcomes.

This integration of awareness and action is what separates wishful thinking from empowered manifestation. You don't just hope for change, you observe it into being.

Conclusion: You Are the Observer and the Creator

The Observer Effect reveals a profound truth: what you observe, you influence. But what you observe with clarity, emotion, and intention, you create. This isn't just science. It's the foundational principle behind every personal transformation and success story.

You've learned that mindfulness allows you to step out of autopilot and into conscious living. You've seen how your thoughts, emotions, and actions shape your reality. And now, you know that to create a different future, you must observe differently today.

Through intentional observation, you are not just watching life happen. You are sculpting it. Your awareness is the brush, your intention the paint, and the quantum field your canvas.

So ask yourself:

"What am I observing into existence today?"

Because the life you seek is not waiting for you in the distance. It is responding to the gaze of your awareness, right now.

In the next chapter, we will explore how your personal energy field interacts with the greater quantum field through the lens of **resonance, frequency, and vibration**. Get ready to uncover the science behind the Law of Attraction, and how to use it deliberately to attract the life you desire.

Chapter 5

Quantum Fields: The Science Behind the Law of Attraction

5. Introduction: Tuning Into the Invisible Force That Shapes Your Reality

Imagine walking into a dark room and flipping a light switch. Instantly, the entire space is illuminated, not because you created the light, but because you tapped into an existing source of energy. Your life works the same way. When you align with the quantum fields that surround and permeate your existence, you unlock profound power, the ability to illuminate the path to your greatest dreams.

Consider the legendary physicist Albert Einstein, who famously said, "Everything is energy and that's all there is to it. Match the frequency of the reality you want and you cannot help but get that reality." Einstein wasn't merely offering poetic wisdom; he deeply understood that reality is woven from invisible quantum fields responsive to energetic resonance. Modern quantum physics now supports this insight, confirming that at the most fundamental level, everything, including you, is energy vibrating at specific frequencies.

You constantly interact with this universal quantum field, knowingly or unknowingly. Every thought, emotion, and belief you hold broadcasts a unique vibrational frequency into the universe, influencing what you attract into your life. The critical question is this: Are you consciously choosing the energetic signals you send out, or are you allowing unconscious patterns to shape your reality?

The path to manifesting your desires goes beyond mere positive thinking, it lies in intentionally aligning your energy with the frequencies of your aspirations. This chapter dives deep into the scientific foundations of the Law of Attraction, revealing practical strategies to consciously work with quantum fields. By the end, you will not only understand how your energy shapes your world but also possess powerful tools to intentionally manifest your deepest desires.

5.1.   Understanding Quantum Fields: The Invisible Fabric of Reality

Imagine tuning a radio to your favorite station. The music is always there, constantly broadcasting through invisible frequencies. Your radio simply needs to be tuned correctly to receive it clearly. Quantum fields operate similarly, they surround and permeate all existence, responding dynamically to your thoughts, emotions, and actions.

At the quantum level, particles are not solid entities; they're probabilities, potentialities existing as waves of energy until observed. When you intentionally focus your attention, you collapse these waves into tangible experiences. Your reality, therefore, is not fixed, it emerges from the quantum field based on your predominant frequencies.

Think of your mind as a powerful transmitter broadcasting a specific frequency. Like tuning a radio, the frequency you send determines what experiences you attract. High-frequency emotions such as joy, gratitude, and abundance resonate strongly within the quantum field, aligning you with experiences that match these elevated vibrations. Conversely, negative emotions like fear or doubt connect you with realities reflecting those states.

Take a moment now to reflect: What frequency are you broadcasting into the quantum field, and how might shifting it positively impact your life?

Understanding quantum fields and your interaction with them is your first powerful step toward creating intentional, lasting change. As we continue this chapter, you'll learn how to consistently tune your energy to attract and manifest your greatest desires.

5.2.   Quantum Resonance: How Frequency Shapes Your Reality

Quantum resonance is the principle by which your energetic frequency attracts experiences and realities that match it. Just as tuning into a specific radio station allows you to receive its unique broadcast, adjusting your emotional and mental frequency tunes you into distinct experiences within the quantum field.

Every emotion, belief, and intention carries a unique vibrational signature. Joy, love, abundance, and gratitude vibrate at higher frequencies, attracting harmonious and positive outcomes. Conversely, fear, doubt, anger, and resentment emit lower frequencies, resonating with experiences that mirror these challenging states.

Imagine two friends, John and Emily. John consistently practices gratitude and maintains an optimistic outlook, frequently feeling joyful and confident. This high-frequency energy brings him supportive friendships, prosperous career opportunities, and fulfilling personal relationships. Emily, however, regularly feels anxious, uncertain, and doubtful. Despite her efforts, these lower vibrational emotions keep her stuck in patterns of financial struggles, strained relationships, and missed opportunities. Their lives vividly reflect the power of quantum resonance.

Your emotional frequency determines the reality you continuously attract. The good news? Your frequency is entirely within your control. You can deliberately choose to broadcast a higher frequency, consciously shaping a reality that matches your highest aspirations.

Interactive Prompt

Pause now and reflect:

"What dominant emotions have you experienced today, and how might these emotions be shaping your reality right now?"

Practical Challenge: The 24-Hour Frequency Shift

Over the next 24 hours, consciously shift your emotional frequency:

1. Start by recalling a recent joyful experience and immerse yourself deeply in those positive feelings.

2. Throughout the day, regularly redirect your thoughts to gratitude, optimism, or joy whenever negative emotions arise.

3. Observe any immediate changes in your interactions, relationships, or opportunities.

By consciously managing your emotional frequency, you harness quantum resonance to attract experiences aligned with your desires, transforming your life one intentional thought at a time.

5.3.   Quantum Fields and Subconscious Beliefs: Your Hidden Architects

Your subconscious mind is like a powerful transmitter, continuously broadcasting your deeply-held beliefs into the quantum field. Whether consciously or unconsciously, these beliefs shape your reality by drawing corresponding experiences into your life, often beyond your immediate awareness.

Beneath your conscious awareness lies a vast collection of subconscious beliefs, built through experiences, culture, upbringing, and self-perceptions, that silently guide your actions, emotions, and outcomes. Quantum fields, highly responsive to emotional frequencies, directly interact with these subconscious signals, manifesting realities that precisely reflect your inner narratives.

Consider Dr. Joseph Murphy, who once carried subconscious beliefs that limited his potential. Despite his conscious aspirations toward success and fulfillment, his hidden fears and doubts unknowingly sabotaged his efforts. Recognizing this pattern, Dr. Murphy began transforming his subconscious beliefs through targeted affirmations and daily visualization practices. Over time, his external circumstances started to shift dramatically; he attracted supportive mentors, lucrative opportunities, and genuine recognition of his abilities.

Interactive Exercise: Identifying Your Beliefs

Pause and honestly reflect on three subconscious beliefs you have about yourself or life. Consider:

1.   How have these beliefs influenced your decisions and experiences?

2.   Are these beliefs empowering or limiting your growth?

Affirmations to Rewrite Your Reality

Commit to integrating these affirmations into your daily routine:

1.   "I effortlessly attract abundance because I deeply believe in my worthiness and potential."

2.   "My subconscious beliefs align perfectly with my dreams, guiding me toward success."

3.   "Every day, my belief system grows stronger, clearer, and more empowering."

By actively reshaping your subconscious beliefs, you leverage the incredible power of quantum fields to manifest a reality aligned with your greatest aspirations.

5.4.   Aligning Your Frequency: Becoming a Conscious Creator

Have you ever wondered why some people seem to effortlessly achieve their dreams, while others consistently struggle despite equal effort? The answer lies in vibrational alignment, the precise synchronization of your thoughts, emotions, and actions with your highest goals.

Imagine alignment as tuning a guitar: even slight misalignment creates discord, but perfect tuning produces harmonious resonance. When your internal energy aligns seamlessly with your external intentions, you resonate clearly with the quantum field, effortlessly attracting matching experiences into your reality.

Take Thomas Edison, whose clear vision of inventing the incandescent light bulb was accompanied by unwavering belief and relentless action. Despite numerous failures, his energetic alignment with success and persistence eventually manifested precisely the outcome he envisioned. His focused intention and emotional frequency created an energetic harmony that made his breakthrough inevitable.

Techniques for Perfecting Your Alignment:

1.   **Visualization Mastery:**

     Spend five minutes daily vividly imagining your desired outcome, engaging all your senses, what you see, feel, hear, and even smell in that achieved state.

2.   **Emotional Frequency Checks:**

     Set reminders throughout your day to pause and assess your emotional frequency. Are your feelings aligned with your intentions? If not, intentionally choose thoughts and emotions that elevate your vibration.

3.   **Alignment-Focused Affirmations:**

     Use affirmations such as:

     1.   "My energy perfectly aligns with the abundance and success I desire."

2.   "I easily and joyfully manifest outcomes aligned with my highest aspirations."

3.   "Every thought and emotion aligns me closer to my dreams."

Reflection Prompts

Pause now and reflect deeply:

1.   What desires are you currently trying to manifest?

2.   Is your energy truly aligned with these intentions, or are there areas of internal discord?

3.   What practical steps can you take today to improve your alignment?

When your inner frequency harmonizes with your outer goals, you step into a powerful flow state, effortlessly manifesting a life reflective of your highest dreams.

5.5.   Daily Quantum Practices: Building Your New Reality

What if dedicating just a few minutes each day could rewrite your life's script, shifting you into a reality filled with abundance, joy, and fulfillment? Your daily habits, when practiced intentionally, become powerful quantum tools that shape your life at an energetic level.

Consider Jim Carrey, who once felt trapped in financial scarcity. He committed himself to just a few minutes of intentional quantum practice each day, visualizing abundance, expressing gratitude, and affirming his prosperity. In a surprisingly short time, he began attracting unexpected financial opportunities, profitable connections, and lucrative projects, transforming his life dramatically.

Your reality is shaped by consistent actions and focused intentions. Here's a practical daily quantum routine you can immediately incorporate into your life:

Daily Quantum Practice Routine:

1. **Morning Visualization (5 minutes):**

   Start each day vividly visualizing your ideal life as if it already exists. Engage all your senses, imagine what you see, hear, feel, and experience in that reality.

2. **Gratitude Amplifier (3 minutes):**

   Write down three genuine reasons for gratitude every morning, immersing yourself in the positive feelings they generate.

3. **Focused Affirmations (3 minutes):**

   Use powerful affirmations such as:

   1. "Every day, my alignment with abundance grows stronger."

   2. "I effortlessly attract opportunities and prosperity through my intentional daily practices."

3. "My consistent daily efforts create clear pathways to success and fulfillment."

4. **Evening Reflection (3 minutes):**

    Each night, reflect briefly on your day's experiences. Acknowledge any positive shifts and identify areas where your alignment can improve.

Reflection and Commitment:

Pause and thoughtfully answer these questions:

1. How committed are you to consistently following this daily quantum practice routine?

2. What significant changes could you anticipate if you fully embrace this quantum habit daily?

Consistency is your gateway to transformation. By adopting these daily quantum practices, you actively engage with the quantum field, consciously shaping your life toward your highest aspirations.

5.6.   Consistent Quantum Interaction: Creating Lasting Change

What would your life look like if you consciously accessed the limitless possibilities of the quantum field every single day? Your consistent daily interactions with this field hold immense power to transform your experiences from the inside out.

Each intention you set, each emotional state you maintain, and each visualization you practice directly interacts with the quantum field, sending clear signals that shape your reality. Through sustained, conscious effort, you align more deeply with the universe's infinite potential, effortlessly drawing in your most cherished dreams.

Actionable Steps for Quantum Consistency:

1. **Daily Intentions:**

    Begin each day by setting clear, focused intentions. Clearly articulate what you wish to manifest and why it's important to you.

2. **Emotional Alignment Checks:**

    Regularly assess your emotional state throughout the day. Consciously elevate your frequency whenever you notice a dip in energy or positivity.

3. **Visualize Daily:**

    Commit to visualizing your goals as achieved for at least a few minutes daily, reinforcing your connection to the quantum field.

Empowering Affirmations:

Incorporate these affirmations into your daily quantum practices:

1. "I am deeply connected to the quantum field and effortlessly manifest my highest potential."

2. "My consistent daily interactions with the quantum field create rapid, positive shifts in my life."

Reflection and Commitment Prompts:

Pause and reflect:

1.   How can you integrate daily quantum interactions seamlessly into your existing routines?

2.   What immediate positive outcomes do you envision from this commitment?

Consistent quantum interaction is your key to lasting change. Embrace these practices and watch your life shift dramatically into alignment with your highest aspirations.

Conclusion: Resonating with the Field of Possibility

You are not separate from the universe, you are a field of energy interacting with a greater field of energy. The Law of Attraction is not simply about thinking positively; it's about embodying a state of resonance that aligns with the reality you wish to experience.

Throughout this chapter, you've discovered that the quantum field responds to energy, not words. Thoughts are important, but it's the vibration behind the thoughts that carries the true signal. By mastering your inner frequency, through emotion, belief, visualization, and aligned action, you become a powerful transmitter, drawing in experiences that mirror your inner state.

You've also seen how resonance is not magic; it's a measurable, repeatable principle of energy alignment. The people, opportunities, and outcomes that appear in your life are responses to the signal you're emitting. And that signal is completely within your control.

As you move forward, remember:

1.   **Your thoughts set the intention.**

2.   **Your emotions charge the energy.**

3.   **Your actions anchor the reality.**

You don't have to force attraction; you simply have to match it.

In the next chapter, we'll expand this idea beyond the individual self and explore the phenomenon of entanglement. You'll discover how your energy doesn't operate in isolation, but is intricately connected with others, and how relationships and collaborations become powerful amplifiers of quantum manifestation when they are energetically aligned.

Prepare to embrace the interconnected nature of reality, and step into the power of collective coherence.

Chapter 6

Entanglement: Embracing Universal Interconnectedness

6. Introduction: The Web of Connection

What if every thought you had, every emotion you felt, and every intention you set were not isolated events but strands in an invisible web connecting you to everything and everyone? This is not just a poetic metaphor, it's a principle grounded in both ancient wisdom and modern quantum physics.

Quantum entanglement, one of the most mind-bending discoveries in physics, suggests that two particles can become linked in such a way that their states instantly affect each other, regardless of the distance between them. Scientists have observed entangled particles interacting across vast distances, defying conventional understandings of space and time. The famous Bell Test experiments and Alain Aspect's groundbreaking research confirmed that these connections exist beyond our classical understanding of cause and effect.

But what if this principle extends beyond the quantum world? What if your energy, your thoughts, emotions, and beliefs, entangles you with people, opportunities, and experiences?

Consider a simple but profound experience: You suddenly think of an old friend you haven't spoken to in years, and moments later, they send you a message. Or you vividly imagine a specific career opportunity, and within days, an unexpected opening appears. Are these mere coincidences, or could they be evidence of an underlying connection shaping your reality?

The reality you experience is not random; it is shaped by the energetic connections you maintain. This chapter explores how you are constantly influencing and being influenced by the unseen web of reality and how you can use this awareness to consciously align with the life you desire.

6.1. Understanding Quantum Entanglement and Human Connection

In traditional physics, cause and effect follow a linear path, one event leads to another in a predictable sequence. However, quantum physics disrupts this notion, revealing that connections can exist outside of time and space.

Entanglement occurs when two particles are so deeply linked that a change in one instantly affects the other, even if they are separated by galaxies. This principle suggests that reality is far more interconnected than we once believed. The groundbreaking Bell Test experiments confirmed this phenomenon, showing that no hidden local variables could explain entangled particles' behavior. Alain Aspect's experiments further proved that entangled particles behave as a single unified system, even when vast distances separate them.

Now, let's apply this to your own life.

Have you ever thought about someone, only for them to call or text you out of the blue? Have you ever had a sudden insight or gut feeling that led you to an unexpected opportunity? These experiences hint at an unseen field of connection, a field in which your thoughts, emotions, and intentions ripple outward, influencing what you attract and what shows up in your reality.

This is not just wishful thinking; it is a reflection of how the energy you emit interacts with the world. The same way two entangled particles influence each other across vast distances, your personal energy, your dominant thoughts and emotions, creates ripples that shape your external experiences.

By understanding this invisible entanglement, you can begin to consciously direct your energy and influence the circumstances of your life. The key is awareness: recognizing that your internal state is always in dialogue with the universe.

Throughout this chapter, we will explore how to shift this dialogue in your favor, ensuring that the entanglements you cultivate align with the reality you desire.

6.2.   The Emotional Frequency of Entanglement

If quantum entanglement explains how things are connected, then emotional frequency explains what you remain entangled with.

Your emotions are not just fleeting feelings; they are vibrational signals that determine what you continuously attract. If you are stuck in low-vibrational emotions, fear, anxiety, self-doubt, you remain energetically entangled with experiences that reinforce those states. But if you shift to higher emotional frequencies, gratitude, joy, self-confidence, you realign with a new set of circumstances.

The Science Behind Emotional Frequency

Neuroscientific research has shown that emotions influence brainwave activity, which in turn affects the electromagnetic field generated by your heart and brain. Studies in heart-brain coherence, conducted by the HeartMath Institute, demonstrate that elevated emotional states such as gratitude and love create stable, harmonious energy fields, while negative emotions generate erratic, disruptive signals. This suggests that emotions are not just internal experiences but also external signals that shape our interactions with the world.

Real-World Examples of Emotional Entanglement

Consider Oprah Winfrey: Oprah has openly discussed her struggles with poverty during her childhood. Growing up in rural Mississippi, she faced significant financial hardship and emotional challenges. Despite these difficulties, she shifted her emotional frequency by focusing on education, self-improvement, and gratitude. Her transformation led to a successful career and immense financial prosperity.

Or take Michelle Obama: Michelle Obama has spoken about the emotional challenges she faced in her marriage with Barack Obama, especially during his presidency. She emphasized the importance of self-love, communication, and mutual respect in overcoming these challenges and maintaining a strong, fulfilling relationship.

The takeaway? Your emotional frequency determines what you remain connected to. If you shift your emotional state, you shift your reality.

6.3.   Subconscious Beliefs and Emotional Setpoints

Beneath your emotions lies something even more powerful, your subconscious mind, the driving force behind your emotional setpoint.

Your subconscious is like a program running in the background, dictating your habitual thoughts and feelings. If it is filled with limiting beliefs, such as "money is hard to come by" or "I am not good enough", then no matter how much you consciously desire success or happiness, your dominant emotional setpoint will pull you back to patterns of scarcity or self-doubt.

The Neuroscience of Subconscious Programming

The subconscious mind operates through neural pathways reinforced by repetition. The brain's plasticity means that frequently repeated thoughts and beliefs create strong neural connections, making those patterns automatic over time. Research in cognitive psychology and neuroplasticity suggests that through conscious effort, new pathways can be formed, effectively rewiring the brain to support more empowering beliefs.

Steps to Rewire Your Subconscious and Shift Your Entanglements

1. **Identify Limiting Beliefs** – Notice patterns in your life. What recurring struggles do you face? What inner narratives do you repeat?

2. **Reprogram Your Mind** – Use affirmations, hypnosis, or meditation to overwrite limiting beliefs with empowering ones.

3. **Consistently Shift Your Emotional State** – Surround yourself with high-vibrational influences, positive environments, supportive people, and empowering content.

4. **Practice Visualization and Emotion Pairing** – Engage in mental imagery where you not only see

but feel yourself experiencing the reality you desire. This strengthens the neural connections associated with those beliefs.

When you change your subconscious programming, you change the frequency you emit, and in turn, you realign with new outcomes.

6.4. Conscious Influence: Shaping Your Energetic Connections

Now that you understand the power of emotional frequency and subconscious beliefs, it's time to take full control of what and whom you are entangled with.

The truth is, whether you realize it or not, you are always influencing and being influenced by the energies around you. Every thought, emotion, and action sends out a vibrational signal, reinforcing the connections that shape your reality. The key to transformation lies in becoming conscious of these interactions so that you can intentionally direct them toward the life you want to create.

Steps to Strengthen Positive Entanglement

1. **Mindful Observation: Tuning Into Your Energy Field**
   Just as quantum particles respond to observation, your reality responds to the energy you emit. Regularly assess your dominant thoughts and emotions. Ask yourself:

   1. *Does my energy align with my goals and desires?*

2.   *Am I sending out signals of abundance or scarcity?*

3.   *What emotions do I repeatedly reinforce?*

Keeping a journal can help track recurring patterns and identify areas where adjustments are needed.

2.   **Conscious Association: Aligning with Supportive Energies**
Your environment and relationships play a crucial role in maintaining your energetic frequency. If you consistently surround yourself with negativity, doubt, or toxic influences, they will entangle with your subconscious and reinforce limiting beliefs. Instead:

1.   Cultivate relationships with people who inspire and uplift you.

2.   Engage with content (books, podcasts, videos) that fuels your growth.

3.   Reduce exposure to fear-based media that triggers stress and lowers your vibration.

Every interaction is an energetic exchange, choose wisely.

3.   **Emotional Mastery: Becoming an Anchor of Stability**
Learning to regulate your emotions ensures that external circumstances do not dictate your internal state. Tools for mastering emotional stability include:

1.   **Meditation** – Trains your mind to remain centered regardless of external triggers.

2.   **Breathwork** – Techniques like deep breathing and box breathing help restore inner calm.

3.   **Mindfulness** – Keeps you present, preventing past regrets or future anxieties from controlling your energy.

When you master your emotions, you no longer react to life, you shape it.

4.   **Energetic Intention Setting: Directing the Flow of Reality**
Before entering any situation, whether a business meeting, a social gathering, or even your morning routine, set a clear energetic intention. Your thoughts act as a tuning fork, adjusting your frequency to align with the reality you want to create.

1.   **Visualize the desired outcome.** What energy do you want to bring? How do you want to feel?

2.   **Affirm your presence.** Say to yourself, *I radiate confidence, abundance, and positivity.*

3.   **Trust the quantum field.** The more deliberate you are with your energy, the more reality shifts in your favor.

Your Influence is Constant, Make it Conscious

You are already entangled with countless energies, shaping your experiences in real-time. By becoming intentional about your thoughts, emotions, and associations, you can direct this entanglement to align with your highest potential.

Every thought is a ripple. Every interaction is a choice. Every moment is an opportunity to shift. Choose wisely, and watch your reality transform.

6.5.   The 7-Day Emotional Mastery Challenge

Mastering your emotional frequency is not a one-time effort but a continuous practice. To help you apply these concepts in a structured way, here's a **7-day challenge** designed to shift your emotional baseline, elevate your vibrational frequency, and observe how your reality responds.

Each day focuses on a specific aspect of emotional mastery, reinforcing your ability to consciously direct your energy and create intentional entanglements.

Day 1: Awareness, Recognizing Your Emotional Patterns

1.   Spend the day simply **observing** your dominant emotional state.

2.   Notice patterns in your thoughts. Do you often feel anxious, frustrated, or doubtful? Or do you naturally gravitate toward gratitude, confidence, and optimism?

3.   Journal your recurring thoughts and emotions, particularly the ones that **drain your energy** or reinforce limiting beliefs.

Day 2: Intentional Gratitude, Rewiring for Positivity

1.   Write down **ten things** you are grateful for and reflect deeply on each.

2.   Throughout the day, engage in **conscious gratitude**, pause and acknowledge small positive moments (e.g., a kind gesture, a beautiful sunset, a good meal).

3.   Gratitude shifts your energetic field, making you receptive to abundance.

Day 3: Emotional Detox, Removing Energetic Blockages

1.   Identify sources of **negative energy** in your life, stressful news, social media, toxic conversations.

2.   Reduce your exposure to negativity by **unfollowing, muting, or limiting** interactions that lower your vibration.

3.   Replace negativity with **high-frequency inputs**, uplifting books, positive affirmations, and calming music.

Day 4: Visualization, Activating Your Future Reality

1.   Spend **10 minutes** visualizing your ideal life in vivid detail.

2.   Engage all your senses, what does this reality **look, feel, sound, and smell** like?

3.   Emotionalize the experience as if it's happening **now**, this strengthens your energetic entanglement with your desired reality.

Day 5: Acts of High Vibration, Expanding Positive Entanglement

1.   Perform **at least three acts of kindness** (e.g., helping someone, offering a genuine compliment, donating).

2.   Observe how these actions **affect your mood** and external interactions.

3.   When you uplift others, you raise your own vibration and attract **higher-quality connections**.

Day 6: Rewriting Subconscious Beliefs, Breaking Old Patterns

1.   Identify **one limiting belief** you hold about yourself (e.g., *I am not good at making money* or *I don't deserve love*).

2.   Challenge it with **an empowering alternative** (e.g., *I attract financial opportunities easily* or *I am worthy of deep, fulfilling relationships*).

3.   Repeat this affirmation **multiple times throughout the day** and write it down.

Day 7: Reflection and Integration, Strengthening Emotional Mastery

1.　　　Reflect on the emotional shifts you've experienced over the past week.

2.　　　Identify the **most powerful insights** and commit to maintaining your new emotional baseline.

3.　　　Create a **personalized emotional mastery plan** to integrate these practices into your daily life.

The Power of Small Shifts

By the end of this challenge, you will have consciously reshaped your **emotional setpoint** and realigned your energy with a higher frequency. Even small shifts in emotional mastery can create profound changes in your reality.

You are not just reacting to life, you are designing it.

6.6.　　Reflection Prompts for Self-Evaluation

True transformation begins with self-awareness. As you embrace the concept of entanglement and its role in shaping your reality, it's essential to reflect on how your thoughts, emotions, and beliefs have influenced your experiences. Use the following prompts to deepen your understanding and align yourself with the energy of your highest potential:

1.　　　**What emotions do I most frequently experience, and how do they shape my reality?**

Are my dominant emotions positive and expansive, or do they reinforce limitation and fear?

2.   **What past experiences have reinforced my current emotional setpoint?**

Have I unknowingly remained entangled with past events that no longer serve me?

3.   **How can I shift my subconscious beliefs to align with my highest self?**

What narratives about myself, success, or happiness need to be reprogrammed?

4.   **What signs of synchronicity have I noticed in my life, and what do they reveal about my entanglements?**

Have I experienced meaningful coincidences that point to the power of unseen connections?

5.   **How can I be more intentional about the energy I emit daily?**

What practices can I incorporate to ensure I radiate the frequency of my desires?

Journaling your responses to these questions will help you recognize recurring patterns, gain new insights, and identify opportunities to shift your energy. The more intentional you become about what you project into the world, the more effectively you will realign with the reality you wish to create.

Conclusion: Living in the Web of Connection

Quantum entanglement reminds us that separation is a story we've been taught, but not the truth of who we are. Beneath the visible threads of everyday life lies a deeper reality: a unified field where every thought, emotion, and intention reverberates through the collective whole. You are not alone in your journey, your energy is always in dialogue with the universe.

In this chapter, you've seen that your inner world doesn't end at the edges of your skin. It reaches outward, touching people, opportunities, and possibilities. The connections you form, whether through love or fear, shape the quality of your life and the direction of your path.

You are not simply living in the world; you are co-creating it, moment by moment.

Every interaction is an echo of your energetic signature. When you shift your vibration, you don't just change what you experience, you change what is possible for everyone entangled with you. That's the power of conscious resonance. That's the ripple of awakened living.

So ask yourself: What are you entangled with today? Old patterns of survival or new frequencies of growth and expansion?

This chapter is your invitation to disentangle from limitations and re-attune to your highest self. Align with the energy of clarity, compassion, abundance, and bold vision. The quantum field is listening, and it responds to what you radiate.

In the next chapter, we'll explore how to navigate the unknown with courage and creativity. You'll learn to not only

withstand uncertainty, but to welcome it, as a sacred threshold where transformation begins and the impossible becomes your new normal.

Chapter 7

The Uncertainty Principle: Thriving in the Unknown

7. Introduction

Life is unpredictable. No matter how much we plan, strategize, or analyze, there will always be factors beyond our control. But what if uncertainty wasn't something to fear, but rather a hidden advantage? What if embracing the unknown was the key to unlocking new opportunities and manifesting success?

In quantum physics, the **Heisenberg Uncertainty Principle** states that we cannot simultaneously know both the exact position and momentum of a particle. The mere act of observation influences reality. This principle has profound implications, not just for science, but for our daily lives. It suggests that reality is not fixed; it is shaped by perception, choices, and energy.

Consider this: Some of the most successful individuals in history did not wait for perfect conditions to act. **Elon Musk** took enormous risks with Tesla and SpaceX, navigating uncharted territory. **Oprah Winfrey** built a media empire despite immense challenges and unknown outcomes. **Jeff Bezos** left a stable career to launch Amazon, venturing into uncertainty with no guarantees.

What set them apart? They **thrived in the unknown**. They understood that uncertainty is not a roadblock but a gateway to possibility.

This chapter will show you how to embrace uncertainty as a tool for transformation, make bold decisions without fear, and tap into the limitless potential of the quantum field. By shifting your mindset, you will no longer resist uncertainty, you will harness it to create your ideal future.

7.1. The Quantum View of Uncertainty

At the heart of reality lies uncertainty. Science tells us that uncertainty is not a flaw or a weakness, it is an inherent feature of existence. The **Uncertainty Principle**, discovered by Werner Heisenberg, suggests that at the quantum level, particles do not have fixed properties until observed. They exist in a state of **superposition**, multiple possibilities at once, until they interact with consciousness.

This mirrors our own lives. The future is not set in stone; it exists as a range of possibilities, influenced by our focus, beliefs, and actions. Just as quantum particles respond to observation, our reality **responds to our mindset and choices.**

Reframing Uncertainty: From Fear to Possibility

Many people resist uncertainty because it feels like chaos. But what if we reframed it as a **playground of potential?** Throughout history, some of the greatest breakthroughs came from uncertainty:

1. **Elon Musk** ignored traditional industry skepticism and pursued electric vehicles and space travel against all odds.

2. **Oprah Winfrey** faced career instability early on but followed her instincts, building an empire.

3. **Jeff Bezos** stepped into the unknown, leaving a stable job to create the world's largest online retailer.

These visionaries didn't wait for certainty, they acted in the face of it. The unknown was not an obstacle; it was an **invitation to create**.

Exercise: Embracing Uncertainty as a Strength

Think of an area in your life where uncertainty is holding you back. **What if you viewed it as an open doorway instead of a dead end?** Write down one way uncertainty could work in your favor. Then, take one small action based on that new perspective.

7.2.   Mastering the Art of Decisive Action

Uncertainty often leads to **paralysis by analysis**, the tendency to overthink, second-guess, and avoid taking action. The fear of making the wrong choice can leave us stuck, waiting for the "perfect" moment. However, science and experience show that decisive action, even in the face of the unknown, creates momentum, unlocks new opportunities, and ultimately shapes reality.

The Quantum Physics of Action

At the quantum level, particles exist in multiple states simultaneously, represented by a **wave function**, a field of probabilities. However, the moment an observer measures a particle, its wave function **collapses** into a definite state. In other words, **observation transforms potential into reality**.

The same principle applies to your life. When you hesitate, your future remains undefined, filled with possibilities but no concrete outcomes. The moment you **make a decision and take action,** you collapse the field of potential into a specific result, shaping your reality.

"In any moment of decision, the best thing you can do is the right thing,
the next best thing is the wrong thing, and the worst thing you can do   is   nothing."
- Theodore Roosevelt

How to Take Action Despite Uncertainty

Decisive action is not about always having the right answers, it's about moving forward even when you don't. Here's how to break free from hesitation and act with confidence:

1. **Focus on the Next Step, Not the Whole Journey** – Trying to predict every outcome can be overwhelming. Instead, focus on what you can do **right now**. One step leads to another, creating a natural path forward.

2. **Make Small, Low-Risk Decisions Quickly** – Develop a habit of quick decision-making in small matters. This strengthens your ability to navigate bigger uncertainties with ease.

3. **Reframe Fear as Excitement** – Physiologically, fear and excitement trigger the same response (increased heart rate, heightened awareness). By consciously **relabeling fear as excitement**, you shift into a state of confidence.

4. **Trust That You Can Adapt** – The need for certainty often stems from a fear of failure. But failure is rarely final. **You can pivot, adjust, and learn along the way,** as long as you keep moving.

Try This: The 5-Minute Decision Challenge

Take a decision you've been postponing and set a 5-minute timer. Use that time to weigh your options, then **commit** to a choice. Trust your gut and take immediate action, whether it's sending an email, making a call, or starting a new project. **The more you practice quick decision-making, the more natural it becomes.**

7.3. The Power of Letting Go

The need for control is deeply ingrained in human nature. We crave certainty, structure, and predictability because they give us a sense of security. However, attempting to control every outcome often leads to **stress, frustration, and limited potential**. The paradox of success is that **true power comes from learning to let go**, not from forcing outcomes, but from trusting the process.

Quantum Surrender: The Science of Letting Go

At the quantum level, particles exist in a state of **superposition,** they hold multiple possibilities until observed. This means reality is not rigid; it unfolds based on interaction and intention. When we let go of rigid expectations, we allow for **better possibilities to emerge** than we could have planned.

A famous example of quantum surrender is **Thomas Edison's invention of the light bulb.** He did not rigidly insist on a single approach; he conducted thousands of experiments, adapting each time. **By embracing uncertainty rather than resisting it, he unlocked innovation.**

The same applies to life. When you stop trying to **control every variable**, you open yourself to synchronicities, hidden opportunities, and creative solutions that were previously invisible.

How to Cultivate Trust in the Unknown

Instead of fighting uncertainty, **lean into it**. Here's how:

1. **Practice Detachment** – Set a clear intention, but release attachment to exactly how or when it happens. This prevents frustration and opens space for unexpected breakthroughs.

2. **Embrace Experimentation** – See life as a series of experiments. Some efforts will succeed, others won't, but all will **teach valuable lessons**.

3. **Use "What If" Questions Positively** – Instead of "What if I fail?" ask, "What if this turns out better than I imagined?" This small shift transforms fear into possibility.

4. **Develop a 'Flow State' Mindset** – Peak performers, from athletes to artists, achieve their best results by being in **flow**, a state of relaxed focus where they trust their instincts instead of overanalyzing.

Try This: The Surrender Experiment

Pick an area of your life where you feel stuck or frustrated due to uncertainty. For the next **seven days**, practice **intentional surrender**, meaning:

1. Set a goal, but let go of controlling the exact outcome.

2. Take inspired action without obsessing over results.

3. Watch for unexpected opportunities that arise.

You'll be surprised how often solutions emerge **when you stop forcing them.**

7.4. Rewiring Your Mind for Uncertainty

Your brain is wired to seek certainty. It craves patterns, predictability, and familiar outcomes because these create a sense of security. This is a survival mechanism, our ancestors depended on recognizing patterns in nature to avoid danger. However, in today's fast-changing world, this hardwiring can be **a major limitation.** The ability to **adapt, embrace uncertainty, and reframe challenges** is the key to personal growth and success.

The good news? **Your brain is not fixed.** Thanks to **neuroplasticity,** you can train your mind to thrive in uncertainty, shifting from fear to confidence.

The Neuroscience of Uncertainty

Studies in neuroscience show that the brain's **amygdala** (which processes fear) becomes highly active when facing the unknown. However, when people **intentionally expose themselves to** uncertainty, they build **new neural pathways**, strengthening their ability to handle unpredictable situations.

In quantum mechanics, particles exist in **a field of potentiality** until they interact with their environment. Similarly, when you rewire your brain to embrace uncertainty, you shift your perception from **fear of the unknown** to **openness to possibility**.

Steps to Build Mental Flexibility

You can train your brain to feel **comfortable in the unknown** by gradually exposing it to uncertainty. Try these techniques:

1. **Expose Yourself to Uncertainty Regularly** – Take small, calculated risks daily. Try a new restaurant, take a different route to work, or start a conversation with a stranger. Small challenges build confidence for bigger ones.

2. **Practice Mindfulness** – Staying present reduces the tendency to overanalyze the future. Meditating for just **5-10 minutes daily** helps calm the amygdala, increasing mental clarity.

3. **Use Visualization Techniques** – Imagine yourself handling uncertainty with ease. Athletes and CEOs use this technique to train their brains for **confidence in unpredictable situations**.

4. **Develop a Growth Mindset** – Instead of seeing challenges as threats, view them as **opportunities for learning and evolution**. Remind yourself that setbacks are **not failures, but feedback**.

Try This: The 24-Hour Uncertainty Challenge

For the next **24 hours**, make a conscious effort to **step into uncertainty**:

1. Say **yes** to something outside your comfort zone.

2. If a plan changes unexpectedly, **embrace it rather than resist it.**

3. Observe how your mind reacts, and choose curiosity over fear.

By consistently practicing **small acts of uncertainty**, your brain **rewires itself** to see the unknown **not as a threat, but as an opportunity for expansion.**

7.5.   Intuition: Your Inner Guide Through Uncertainty

Uncertainty can be daunting, but what if you had an **inner compass** that could guide you through it with confidence? That compass is **intuition**, your ability to sense the best path forward, even when logic does not provide clear answers.

Many of history's greatest minds, **Albert Einstein, Nikola Tesla, Steve Jobs, and Oprah Winfrey**, have credited intuition as a key force behind their decisions. Einstein famously said, **"The intuitive mind is a sacred gift and the rational mind is a faithful servant."** Intuition is not irrational; it is a **powerful form of intelligence** that operates beyond conscious reasoning.

By strengthening your intuition, you become better equipped to **navigate uncertainty, make aligned decisions, and manifest success faster.**

The Quantum Science of Intuition

Quantum physics reveals that **particles can be instantaneously connected across vast distances**, a phenomenon known as **quantum entanglement**. Some scientists suggest that **human consciousness may function in a similar way**, allowing us to access insights beyond our immediate environment.

This could explain why:

1. You sometimes **"just know" something** before it happens.

2. You get a **gut feeling** about an opportunity, whether to pursue it or walk away.

3. You think about someone, and then they **suddenly call or message you**.

These experiences suggest that **intuition is real, and it is backed by science**. The key is learning how to trust and strengthen it.

Developing a Stronger Intuitive Sense

Intuition is like a muscle, the more you use it, the stronger it becomes. Here are five ways to **sharpen your intuitive abilities**:

1. **Quiet the Noise** – Your intuition speaks in whispers, not shouts. Spend time in silence, meditation, or nature to hear it more clearly.

2. **Listen to Your Body** – Science shows that gut instincts are real, your nervous system picks up on patterns before your conscious mind does. Pay attention to how your body reacts to decisions.

3. **Ask and Trust** – When facing uncertainty, ask yourself, **"What feels most aligned?"** Instead of overanalyzing, trust the first feeling that arises.

4. **Look for Synchronicities** – The universe often communicates through signs, pay attention to repeating numbers, coincidences, and intuitive nudges.

5. **Act on Your Hunches** – The more you follow your intuition, the more you prove to yourself that it works. Even small intuitive decisions build trust in your inner guidance.

Try This: The 5-Second Rule for Intuitive Action

The next time you feel an **intuitive nudge**, count down **5...4...3...2...1** and act before doubt creeps in. This simple trick, used by peak performers, helps bypass overthinking and allows intuition to lead.

Intuition and Success: The Stories We Know

Highly successful individuals frequently rely on intuition to make critical decisions:

1. **Steve Jobs** trusted his instincts when designing Apple's products, focusing on what felt right rather than just data.

2. **Oprah Winfrey** consistently emphasizes how following her gut feeling led her to major breakthroughs in her career.

3. **Richard Branson** often says that some of his best business moves were based on instinct, rather than analysis.

The lesson? The most successful people do not wait for **perfect certainty**, they trust their **inner knowing** and move forward with confidence.

Your Inner GPS in an Uncertain World

Uncertainty will never disappear completely, but your ability to **navigate it with ease** can grow stronger. When you trust your intuition, you unlock an internal guidance system that leads you to the right people, opportunities, and decisions, often **faster than logic alone could**.

The next chapter will build on this idea by exploring **how to activate your quantum potential to turn dreams into reality**. By merging trust, action, and intuition, you will step into the full power of **manifesting success with precision and confidence**.

7.6. The Bridge to Quantum Potentiality

Thriving in uncertainty is not just about acceptance, it's about using it as a stepping stone to unlock limitless possibilities. The moment you stop resisting the unknown and instead flow with it, you step into what quantum physicists call the **field of infinite potentiality**.

The Quantum Leap: From Uncertainty to Manifestation

In quantum mechanics, a wave function represents all possible states of a particle until it is observed, at which point it collapses into a specific reality. This principle suggests that:

1. Every moment of uncertainty holds multiple possible outcomes.

2. Your focus, beliefs, and actions determine which reality materializes.

3. When you embrace uncertainty rather than fear it, you open the door to greater possibilities than you could logically predict.

This means that uncertainty isn't something to avoid, it's the gateway to quantum potentiality, where you can create and manifest beyond perceived limitations.

How to Leverage Uncertainty for Quantum Growth

1. **Shift Your Perception: See Uncertainty as a Gift**
   Instead of viewing the unknown as dangerous, reframe it as an exciting space of potential. Many of life's biggest breakthroughs happen outside of predictability.

2. **Take Inspired Action, Even Without Guarantees**
   The act of moving forward, even with incomplete information, collapses possibilities into reality. Trust that every step reveals the next.

3. **Remain Open to Unseen Possibilities**
   Just as quantum particles exist in multiple states before being observed, your future holds multiple versions of success. Stay open to paths you haven't considered yet.

4. **Trust That the Universe Works in Your Favor**
   The energy you send out, through thoughts, emotions, and actions, directly influences what unfolds. Faith in the process creates alignment with better outcomes.

Try This: The "Embrace the Unknown" Challenge

For the next 7 days, do something daily that puts you in a space of positive uncertainty:

1. Say yes to an unexpected opportunity.
2. Make a decision without overanalyzing.
3. Step outside your comfort zone in some way.

Reflect on how these actions shift your confidence in handling uncertainty.

Conclusion: The Power of Thriving in the Unknown

By now, you've uncovered the profound truth that uncertainty is not an obstacle, it is the very fabric of creation. Every moment of doubt, every unexpected turn, and every unknown path is a doorway to greater possibilities. Quantum physics has shown us that nothing is truly fixed until observed, and the same applies to your reality: **it remains fluid until you define it through thought, intention, and action.**

When you master the ability to thrive in uncertainty:

1.   You step into a realm where new opportunities appear effortlessly.

2.   You develop unshakable inner confidence, knowing that the unknown is your ally.

3.   You free yourself from the illusion of control and embrace the magic of unfolding possibilities.

This chapter has equipped you with the tools to navigate uncertainty with ease, tap into your intuition, and take inspired action even when the path isn't clear. You are no longer a passive observer in life, you are an active creator, shaping your destiny moment by moment.

Bridging into the Next Chapter: Quantum Potentiality

At this point, you've learned how to navigate uncertainty with confidence, trust your intuition, and take decisive action. Now, you are ready for the next level, **harnessing the quantum field to consciously create your reality.**

In the next chapter, we will explore **Quantum Potentiality**, the science of turning dreams into tangible reality. By applying everything you've learned so far, you'll gain the tools to manifest with precision and confidence.

The unknown isn't something to fear. **It's the gateway to your highest potential.**

Chapter 8

Quantum Potentiality: Manifesting Dreams into Reality

8. Introduction: The Universe as a Field of Infinite Possibilities

Imagine standing in front of a vast ocean, holding a single drop of water in your hand. That drop, while small, contains the same fundamental essence as the boundless sea before you. In the same way, your mind and consciousness are intrinsically connected to the limitless potential of the universe. You are not separate from the creative forces that shape reality, you are an active participant in them.

Consider the story of Jim Carrey, a struggling actor in the early 1990s who wrote himself a check for $10 million for "acting services rendered." He dated it for five years into the future and carried it in his wallet, visualizing his success daily. Almost exactly five years later, he landed a role in *Dumb and Dumber*, with a pay check of $10 million. His belief and focus tapped into quantum potentiality, collapsing probability into reality.

This concept is not just wishful thinking; it is a direct reflection of quantum potential, an underlying field of infinite possibilities that governs the behavior of all things. In quantum physics, reality does not exist in a fixed state but as an ocean of probabilities, only becoming definite when observed or acted upon.

Just as subatomic particles respond to observation, our thoughts, intentions, and actions interact with the quantum field to bring possibilities into reality. The key is learning how to navigate this field effectively. How do we tap into the unseen realm of potential and translate it into tangible experiences? How do we shift from mere dreamers to conscious creators of our destiny?

This chapter explores how to harness quantum potentiality to turn dreams into reality. By understanding how to align with the principles of quantum manifestation, and how to leverage resonance in relationships and collaborations, you can transform abstract desires into concrete experiences, stepping into the full power of conscious creation.

8.1. The Quantum Potential: The Blueprint of Reality

Understanding the Field of Infinite Possibilities

Quantum physics reveals that everything exists in a state of pure potential before it is observed or acted upon. This means that multiple realities exist simultaneously, waiting to be selected through conscious focus and decision-making.

Physicist David Bohm described reality as a two-layered system:

1. **The Implicate Order**: The unseen, underlying field of limitless possibilities where everything is interconnected.

2. **The Explicate Order**: The manifested, physical reality that emerges from the quantum field based on observation and interaction.

Your thoughts, emotions, and beliefs influence how possibilities unfold from the implicate order into your experienced reality. If you learn to focus your awareness, set clear intentions, and take inspired action, you become the architect of your own life.

A striking example of this principle in action comes from Nikola Tesla, one of history's greatest inventors. Before building any device, Tesla would visualize it in complete detail, testing its mechanics in his mind. Only when he was satisfied that it functioned perfectly in his mental simulations would he bring it into the physical world. This method aligns with quantum potentiality, he was selecting a reality from the field of infinite possibilities and bringing it into existence through focus and intention.

The Observer Effect: How Attention Shapes Reality

We have already explored the Observer Effect, where quantum particles exist in multiple states until observed. The same principle applies to personal development and success. What you focus on expands, whether it be opportunities, challenges, abundance, or limitation.

To harness this principle effectively:

1. **Shift from passive observation to intentional focus**, direct your attention to what you want, rather than what you fear.

2. **Use visualization and mental rehearsal**, create a vivid, detailed image of your desired outcome.

3. **Cultivate elevated emotions**, gratitude, joy, and excitement raise your vibrational frequency, aligning you with your desired reality.

By understanding and applying these principles, you can consciously shape your reality, transforming quantum potential into tangible results.

And remember, this potential isn't limited to individual goals. As we'll explore later in this chapter, your energy also influences relationships, collaborations, and the people you attract into your journey of success.

8.2. The Mechanics of Manifestation: Aligning Mind, Emotion, and Action

Step 1: Clarity of Intention

Manifestation begins with defining a clear and conscious intention. The quantum field does not respond to vague hopes; it responds to precise, emotionally charged desires. Like setting coordinates in a GPS, your intention provides a destination for the quantum field to navigate toward.

1. **Be specific**: Clearly articulate what you want in terms of outcomes, feelings, and experiences.

2. **Align with authenticity**: Ensure your desires come from your higher self, not societal conditioning or ego-based fear.

3. **Declare it in writing**: Writing down your goals imprints them in your subconscious and magnetizes your awareness toward opportunities.

Your intention becomes a quantum directive, an energetic command to the universe that initiates the collapse of possibility into form.

Step 2: Emotional Coherence and Belief

Emotion is the frequency carrier of your intention. The quantum field mirrors not just your thoughts, but the energy behind them.

1. **Feel it now**: Generate the emotions of your desired outcome as if it is already real. Your nervous system doesn't know the difference.

2. **Dissolve inner conflict**: Doubt, fear, and second-guessing create static in your frequency. Awareness and release practices such as breathwork, EFT, or journaling can clear these blocks.

3. **Build belief incrementally**: Use affirmations, micro-wins, and visualization to rewire your self-concept and generate emotional momentum.

Think of your intention as a signal and your emotion as the amplifier. Together, they broadcast a frequency that draws your desired outcome into your life.

Step 3: Taking Inspired Quantum Action

Manifestation is not magic, it's co-creation. While the quantum field holds infinite potential, it requires your participation.

1. **Act from alignment**: Let action emerge from inspiration, not obligation. Inspired action feels expansive, not exhausting.

2. **Don't wait for all the answers**: Begin moving in the direction of your desire, and the next steps will appear.

3.   **Embody the version of you who has already arrived**: Make decisions as if you already are the person who has what you want.

Quantum leaps occur when you show up as your future self now. The field responds in kind, adjusting your external reality to match your inner state.

8.3.   Overcoming Resistance: Breaking Through Self-Imposed Limits

Even when your desires are clear, internal resistance can delay or distort your manifestations. Resistance is not failure, it's a signal that there's an energetic mismatch between your current identity and your desired reality.

Common Forms of Resistance:

1.   **Subconscious conditioning**: Limiting beliefs formed early in life often remain unexamined and dictate your energetic baseline.

2.   **Fear of expansion**: Sometimes, we fear the very success we say we want, because it requires us to change, let go, or be seen.

3.   **Clinging to identity**: The familiar, even if painful, can feel safer than the unknown. Resistance often shows up as the ego protecting what it knows.

Strategies to Transmute Resistance:

1.   **Inner Dialogue Auditing:** Pay attention to the narratives running in your mind. Are you affirming

your vision or reinforcing your doubts? Reframe limiting beliefs into empowering truths.

2.   **Embrace Discomfort as Growth:** What feels uncomfortable now may be stretching you into the version of yourself who can hold more abundance, love, or success. Lean into growth edges.

3.   **Energetic Clearing:** Use practices like journaling, breathwork, or guided meditation to release emotional tension and stagnant beliefs. Movement and sound healing can also clear energetic blocks.

4.   **Identity Alignment:** Ask yourself daily: Who am I being? Is this identity congruent with the version of me who already has my desired outcome? Shift accordingly.

5.   **Quantum Accountability:** Surround yourself with people who see and support your highest potential. Collective resonance amplifies personal transformation.

Resistance is part of the path. But once you bring it into awareness and actively choose alignment over fear, you transmute resistance into momentum. The field responds not to perfection, but to your willingness to evolve.

8.4.   The Role of Energy, Vibration, and Resonance in Manifestation

Everything Is Energy

At its core, the quantum universe is vibrational. Every thought, emotion, and intention emits a frequency that interacts with the quantum field. This field doesn't respond to words alone, it responds to energy. The Law of Resonance teaches us that similar frequencies attract one another. You don't manifest what you want; you manifest what you are in energetic resonance with.

Tuning Your Frequency

To manifest your desires, you must become a vibrational match to them.

1. **Elevate Emotional States**

   Practice gratitude, joy, love, and excitement, these are high-frequency states that align with abundance and success.

   Use breathwork, movement, music, or nature to quickly raise your vibrational baseline.

2. **Visualization with Sensory Depth**

   The brain responds to vivid mental imagery. See, hear, and feel your desired reality as if it's happening now.

   Add physical emotion to your practice: smile, breathe deeply, and embody the feeling of success.

3. **Affirmative Identity Statements**

   Speak as the version of yourself who has already received what you seek.

Examples: "I radiate clarity and confidence." "I attract aligned opportunities every day."

4. **Energetic Hygiene**

    Clear energy leaks such as toxic relationships, negative media, and limiting environments.

    Protect your frequency like you would your most valuable asset, because it is.

Relationship Resonance

Your energy not only shapes your personal reality, it affects those around you. In relationships and collaboration, resonance becomes exponential.

1. **Aligned partnerships amplify outcomes**: Two or more people holding a shared vision can manifest with greater speed and harmony.

2. **Entanglement in Action**: Just as entangled particles affect each other instantly, humans who are emotionally and energetically connected can co-create synchronously, even across distance.

3. **Collective Intentionality**: Join or create communities of high-frequency individuals committed to growth. The field created by the group lifts everyone within it.

You are both a transmitter and receiver. When your inner state matches the frequency of your desired life, and you surround yourself with others doing the same, you activate resonance at a quantum level.

8.5. Trusting the Process: The Art of Surrender and Allowing

Let Go to Let In

One of the most counterintuitive but essential aspects of quantum manifestation is surrender. Once you've set a clear intention, aligned emotionally, and taken inspired action, your next move is to allow.

Why Surrender Matters

1. Obsessing over the outcome introduces resistance.

2. Worry and doubt lower your frequency, disrupting resonance.

3. Trust allows the field to reorganize and deliver outcomes in divine timing.

Keys to Mastering the Art of Allowing:

1. **Detach from the "How"**

   Let go of needing to control the path. Your job is clarity; the field's job is orchestration.

   Ask: "Am I trying to force this, or am I trusting my alignment?"

2. **Presence Over Pressure**

   Focus on embodying your future self now, rather than constantly monitoring results.

Live your day with joy, confidence, and faith, as if it's already done.

3. **Celebrate Small Signs**

    Acknowledge every sign of progress, synchronicity, or aligned opportunity.

    These are signals that your intention is crystallizing into form.

4. **Reframe Waiting as Receiving**

    Instead of waiting passively, live expectantly. Each moment is a preparation for your manifestation's arrival.

5. **Daily Surrender Practice**

    Each evening, journal one thing you're letting go of and one thing you're trusting in.

    Affirm: "I am supported by the universe. My desires are unfolding perfectly."

Quantum Truth: The field doesn't respond to desperation; it responds to belief.

By releasing control and remaining in vibrational alignment, you accelerate manifestation. Surrender is not giving up; it's giving space, for the miraculous to unfold.

8.6. Embodying Quantum Potentiality: Becoming a Conscious Creator

The Shift from Passive to Active Manifestation

Understanding quantum potentiality is not just about intellectual knowledge, it is about embodiment. To truly manifest the reality you desire, you must move from being a passive dreamer to an active creator who consistently aligns thoughts, emotions, and actions with your vision.

Most people remain stuck in wishful thinking, hoping for change while maintaining old habits and beliefs. Quantum manifestation requires full immersion, living as though your desired reality is already unfolding.

Daily Practices to Strengthen Manifestation

To fully integrate quantum principles into your life, commit to the following transformative practices:

1. **Morning Reality Creation Ritual**

   Begin each day by visualizing your desired outcomes with strong emotional engagement.

   Speak affirmations that reinforce your new reality.

   Set clear, intentional actions that align with your goals.

2. **Quantum Rehearsal: Acting as If**

   Adopt the habits, mindset, and confidence of the future self you are becoming.

   Shift your internal dialogue to reflect your new reality.

Make decisions based on where you want to be, not where you are now.

3.   **Energetic Alignment and Emotional Mastery**

Keep your vibrational state elevated by practicing gratitude, meditation, and mindfulness.

Transmute negative emotions into growth opportunities rather than allowing them to lower your frequency.

4.   **Trust and Adaptability**

Remain open to unexpected pathways, manifestation often unfolds in ways beyond what the logical mind can predict.

Release resistance and surrender control while staying aligned with your vision.

The Ultimate Realization: You Are the Quantum Field

As you integrate these practices, a profound truth emerges, you are not separate from the quantum field, you are it.

Every thought, emotion, and action you take sends ripples through the vast field of potentiality, shaping reality in ways beyond immediate perception. The more consciously you engage with this field, the more effortlessly your life transforms.

The key is not just to understand quantum potentiality, it is to embody it in every moment.

Conclusion: You Are the Creator of Your Reality

The principle of quantum potentiality teaches us that reality is not something we passively experience, but something we actively shape. By mastering the art of focused intention, emotional alignment, and inspired action, you can manifest your dreams with precision and purpose.

Key Takeaways:

1. Reality exists as a field of limitless potential before it is shaped by observation and choice.

2. Your focus and beliefs determine which possibilities collapse into reality.

3. Manifestation requires clarity, emotional alignment, and action.

4. Overcoming inner resistance is essential to unlocking your full creative power.

Each thought you think, each emotion you cultivate, and each action you take is a brushstroke on the canvas of your existence. The question is: What masterpiece are you creating?

Looking Ahead: The Quantum Mind-Body Connection

Now that you've learned how to manifest through quantum potentiality, it's time to explore the powerful relationship between consciousness and physical health. In the next chapter, *Quantum Healing: Harnessing the Mind-Body Connection*, we'll dive into how your thoughts, emotions, and beliefs can influence your biology and activate your body's natural capacity to heal.

Final Thought: Step Into Your Power

Tonight, before you sleep, close your eyes and step into the version of yourself that has already achieved your dreams. Feel it, believe it, and wake up ready to act on it.

Chapter 9

Quantum Healing: Harnessing the Mind-Body Connection

9. Introduction: The Healing Power Within

What if the most powerful medicine available to you isn't found in a pill or hospital, but within your own mind and energy field?

Imagine a man diagnosed with terminal cancer who, against all odds, experiences complete remission. Doctors call it spontaneous. He calls it belief. Across the world, countless stories like this point to a hidden potential within the human system, one that defies traditional medical logic. What science once dismissed as anecdotal or mystical, quantum physics is beginning to explain.

At the heart of quantum theory lies a revolutionary idea: that everything is made of energy, and that this energy is not passive. It responds to consciousness. Our minds and bodies are not separate machines, but deeply entangled participants in a dynamic energy field. Ancient healing systems have long understood this. Now, modern science is catching up.

This chapter explores **Quantum Healing**, the process of restoring health by working with the body's subtle energy fields and the mind's ability to influence physical matter. You will learn how **thoughts, emotions, beliefs, and awareness** act as frequencies that can either disrupt or restore balance. By aligning these inner forces, you can awaken the body's natural capacity to heal.

We'll explore the science behind mind-body healing, practical techniques you can begin using today, and inspiring stories of transformation. Whether you seek relief from chronic illness, emotional wounds, or simply want to optimize your well-being, quantum healing invites you to become an active participant in your wellness journey.

The healer you've been waiting for might just be you.

9.1.   The Science of Quantum Healing

The Quantum Field and the Body's Blueprint

In quantum physics, all matter is energy vibrating at different frequencies. Your body, your thoughts, and your emotions are not exceptions, they are part of this same energetic fabric. When your energy is in harmony, health flows. When it's disrupted, disease often follows.

Rather than viewing the body as a machine with isolated parts, quantum biology sees the body as an intelligent, **interconnected information system**. Cells communicate not just chemically, but energetically. Thoughts influence biology. Beliefs shift genetic expression. Emotions alter cellular function.

Scientific Breakthroughs Supporting Quantum Healing

1.   **Epigenetics:** Dr. Bruce Lipton's research shows that genes are not destiny. Our environment, thoughts, and emotional state can switch genes on or off, affecting health outcomes.

2.   **The Placebo Effect:** When a patient heals after receiving a sugar pill, belief is the catalyst. This isn't just trickery, it's evidence that the mind can activate biological healing.

3. **Biofield Science:** Research into energy medicine (like Reiki and acupuncture) reveals that manipulating subtle energy fields can reduce pain, improve mood, and accelerate recovery.

How the Mind Influences the Body

1. **Neuroplasticity:** Your brain rewires itself in response to repeated thoughts and experiences. Negative thinking can reinforce stress responses; empowering beliefs can rewire for healing.

2. **Heart-Brain Coherence:** Studies by the HeartMath Institute reveal that positive emotions like gratitude and compassion create physiological harmony, boosting immunity and reducing stress.

3. **Mindfulness and Meditation:** These practices quiet the analytical mind, reduce inflammation, and shift the body into a healing state by promoting parasympathetic nervous system activity.

The Role of Conscious Intention

Just as the observer in quantum experiments collapses a wave into a particle, **your focused attention collapses energetic possibilities into biological outcomes**. Intention is not wishful thinking, it's directional energy. It tells your cells, "This is where we're going."

Key Insight

Healing is not solely about fixing what's broken; it's about restoring harmony to a system that knows how to heal when supported. By aligning your thoughts, emotions, and energy with the frequency of wellness, you unlock your most powerful medicine, yourself.

In the next section, we'll explore the nature of the energy field surrounding and flowing through your body, and how working with it can deepen your healing journey.

9.2.   Energy Fields and the Human Body

The Human Energy System

Your body is more than muscle, bone, and organs, it's also a sophisticated system of energy centers and fields. Across traditions and cultures, this system has been referred to by many names: **chi** in Chinese medicine, **prana** in Ayurveda, and the **biofield** in modern science. Though terminology varies, the idea remains consistent: the body is enveloped and infused with a subtle energy that affects health, consciousness, and vitality.

Within this energetic framework, key components include:

1.   **Chakras:** Spinning energy centers aligned along the spine, each governing specific physical, emotional, and psychological functions.

2.   **Meridians and Nadis:** Pathways through which life force energy flows, analogous to an energetic circulatory system.

3.   **Auric Field:** The electromagnetic energy field surrounding the body, influenced by thoughts, emotions, and environmental factors.

When your energy flows freely and remains balanced, you experience well-being. When it's blocked, stagnant, or disrupted, disease can manifest.

Scientific Exploration of the Biofield

While still a growing field of study, modern science is beginning to validate the existence of the body's energy fields:

1. **Biofield Research:** The National Institutes of Health (NIH) recognizes the biofield as a "massless field, not necessarily electromagnetic, that surrounds and permeates living bodies." Studies suggest that disruptions in this field may precede physical symptoms.

2. **Heart and Brain Electromagnetic Fields:** Your heart generates an electromagnetic field measurable several feet outside the body. Similarly, EEG technology detects the brain's electric activity, both are forms of measurable bioenergetics.

3. **Photonic and Biophoton Emissions:** Research has shown that living cells emit weak light (biophotons), which may play a role in cellular communication and regulation.

This suggests that health and disease may originate not just in the biochemical realm but also in the energetic one.

The Mind-Body-Energy Feedback Loop

Your body, mind, and energy are in constant communication:

1. **Negative emotions** can constrict energy flow, leading to tension and dysfunction.

2. **Positive emotions** like love and joy expand energy fields, promoting healing.

3. **Thoughts and beliefs** act as instructions to your energetic system, influencing the quality and direction of energy.

Practical Insight

Your health is not only the result of what you eat or how you exercise, but also of what you think and feel, daily. Becoming aware of your energy field and learning how to balance it is key to unlocking your innate healing potential.

9.3.   Thoughts, Beliefs, and the Biology of Healing

Your Mind as a Healing Instrument

Every thought carries a frequency, and every belief creates a blueprint that your body follows. Your biology isn't just shaped by genetics but also by the **stories you repeatedly tell yourself.** These stories influence hormones, immunity, cellular repair, and even how genes express themselves.

The Power of Belief

1. **Placebo and Nocebo Effects:** Patients who believe they will heal often do, even with sugar pills, while those who expect side effects can experience them even when receiving neutral treatments.

2. **Psychoneuroimmunology:** This field studies how psychological states affect the nervous and immune systems. Optimism, trust, and purpose can enhance immunity, while chronic stress and pessimism can weaken it.

3. **Faith and Spirituality:** Studies show that people who engage in spiritual practices or have a strong sense of belief often experience faster recovery, lower stress, and higher resilience.

Reprogramming the Healing Narrative

To activate your inner healing, it's vital to challenge disempowering beliefs and replace them with supportive ones:

1. **Awareness:** Notice recurring thoughts like "I'll never get better" or "This is just how I am." These become subconscious programs that your body follows.

2. **Disruption:** Interrupt the cycle. Ask: "Is this belief absolutely true?"

3. **Replacement:** Introduce empowering alternatives like "My body is healing more each day," or "I am open to recovery in unexpected ways."

Visualization and Healing

Visualization is not just imagination, it is a mental rehearsal that imprints instructions into your subconscious and influences biological systems:

1. Athletes use it to enhance performance.

2. Patients who visualize white blood cells attacking cancer or tissues regenerating often experience improved health outcomes.

Consistent imagery, paired with elevated emotion, creates a powerful internal signal that your body responds to as if it were real.

Practical Tip

Take five minutes each day to close your eyes and visualize your body glowing with vitality. See your cells regenerating. Feel health, peace, and energy radiating through you. The more detailed and emotionally vivid the experience, the greater the impact.

Healing begins when your thoughts and beliefs stop resisting wellness and start aligning with it.

9.4. Emotional Energy and Vibrational Healing

Emotions are not merely psychological experiences; they are energetic frequencies that resonate through the body and the quantum field. When you experience emotions like love, gratitude, or joy, your vibrational frequency rises. Conversely, emotions such as fear, resentment, or guilt lower your frequency and create energetic disharmony.

Emotions as Energy in Motion

The word "emotion" itself is derived from the Latin *emotere*, meaning "to move." Emotions are indeed energy in motion. They influence the flow of information and coherence in your body. Positive emotions create internal harmony, allowing your cells to communicate more effectively and fostering physical healing. Negative emotions can cause energetic blockages, manifesting as physical symptoms over time.

Imagine your body as a symphony. When each instrument (organ, cell, system) is in tune, the music is harmonious. But when one instrument is out of sync due to unresolved emotional energy, it disrupts the entire performance. Healing, then, involves restoring this inner harmony.

Scientific Evidence of Emotional Influence on Health

Research by the HeartMath Institute has shown that emotional states influence heart rhythm patterns. Coherent emotions (such as appreciation and compassion) produce smooth, ordered heart rhythms, which enhance immune function and emotional stability. Incoherent emotions (such as frustration and anxiety) create chaotic patterns that disrupt internal balance.

Additionally, studies in psychoneuroimmunology demonstrate that emotional stress weakens the immune system, while positive emotional expression enhances it. These findings affirm that healing is not just biochemical, it is deeply emotional and energetic.

Techniques for Emotional Healing

To facilitate quantum healing, you must learn to process and transmute emotional energy. Here are some practical tools:

1. **Emotional Freedom Technique (EFT):** Also known as tapping, EFT combines acupressure and verbal affirmations to release stuck emotional energy from the body.

2. **Heart Coherence Breathing:** Slow, rhythmic breathing while focusing on the heart area helps shift emotional states and synchronize the heart and brain.

3. **Expressive Writing:** Journaling thoughts and feelings about emotional events helps bring subconscious emotions to the surface and integrate them consciously.

4. **Gratitude Practice:** Regularly expressing gratitude raises your emotional frequency and aligns your energy field with healing.

5. **Forgiveness Visualization:** Imagine releasing resentment or guilt as a form of energetic liberation, restoring balance to your system.

Emotional Mastery as a Healing Gateway

True healing requires emotional courage, the willingness to feel, acknowledge, and release suppressed emotions. When you become emotionally fluent, you clear energetic pathways, allowing your body's natural healing intelligence to flow.

Every thought and feeling sends a signal through your biofield. The more consistently you choose emotional states that align with health, peace, and vitality, the more you entangle with the quantum potential of complete wellness.

Your emotions are not obstacles, they are messengers. Listen to them, learn from them, and let them guide you back into alignment with your highest healing frequency.

9.5. Energy Psychology and the Healing Mind

Energy psychology bridges the gap between emotional healing and energy-based therapies by addressing psychological issues through the body's energy systems. This emerging field works on the premise that trauma, stress, and limiting beliefs are not just mental but are energetically stored within the body, and by shifting these energetic patterns, we can facilitate rapid emotional and physical healing.

The Principles of Energy Psychology

Energy psychology blends modern psychological techniques with the ancient understanding that the body holds emotional energy. The key principles include:

1. **The Body as an Energetic System:** Emotions, thoughts, and trauma are stored not just in the brain, but throughout the body's energetic pathways.

2. **Blockages Lead to Symptoms:** Emotional distress, anxiety, chronic pain, and even illness can often be traced back to unresolved energetic disruptions.

3. **Restoring Flow Promotes Healing:** By clearing blockages and restoring balance to the body's energy systems, healing is accelerated on both emotional and physical levels.

Popular Modalities in Energy Psychology

Several methods within energy psychology have gained recognition for their ability to produce measurable results:

1. **Emotional Freedom Techniques (EFT or "Tapping"):** Combines cognitive reframing with tapping on acupuncture points to reduce stress, release trauma, and reprogram beliefs.

2. **Thought Field Therapy (TFT):** Uses specific tapping sequences to collapse negative emotional patterns linked to trauma or phobias.

3. **Tapas Acupressure Technique (TAT):** Combines acupressure with focused intention to release limiting beliefs and emotional blocks.

4. **Psych-K and ThetaHealing®:** Techniques that reprogram subconscious beliefs by accessing brainwave states aligned with healing and transformation.

These approaches often produce shifts within minutes, suggesting that working with the body's energetic blueprint offers profound results where talk therapy alone may fall short.

Scientific Insights and Emerging Research

While energy psychology is still gaining mainstream scientific acceptance, early studies have shown promising results:

1. **Cortisol Reduction:** A study published in *The Journal of Nervous and Mental Disease* found that a single EFT session significantly reduced cortisol levels (a marker of stress).

2. **Brainwave Repatterning:** EEG studies show that tapping techniques alter brainwave patterns, moving individuals from high-stress beta states to

more relaxed alpha and theta states associated with healing and creativity.

3.   **Clinical Efficacy:** Energy psychology has been successfully used for conditions such as PTSD, anxiety, phobias, depression, and chronic pain.

These findings suggest that integrating energy-based modalities with traditional therapeutic practices can dramatically enhance outcomes and empower individuals to heal from within.

The Mind as the Conductor of Energy

At its core, energy psychology reinforces a central idea in quantum healing: **the mind is not separate from the body, it is the conductor of its energy**. When you learn to direct your awareness and intention toward healing, you activate pathways that can influence your biochemistry, nervous system, and overall vitality.

By integrating energy psychology into your self-healing toolkit, you begin to operate not only as a passive recipient of health care but as a **conscious director of your mind-body system**.

9.6.   Practical Quantum Healing Techniques

If the body is a quantum system and consciousness is its most powerful influence, then true healing must engage the mind, energy, and intention in harmony. This section outlines practical quantum healing techniques that allow you to take charge of your well-being by working with your body's energetic and informational blueprint.

Intention-Focused Visualization

Visualization is more than imagination; it is the focused projection of consciousness into the quantum field.

Practice:

1.   Sit in a quiet space and visualize your body in a perfect state of health.

2.   Engage all senses: See the vibrant cells, feel the vitality, hear your breath flowing with ease.

3.   Say internally: "My body knows how to heal. I am returning to balance."

4.   Repeat daily for at least 10 minutes, especially when dealing with illness or stress.

Why it works: Focused attention collapses potential healing states into reality. Emotionally charged imagery activates physiological responses aligned with the visualization.

Quantum Breathwork

Breath is the bridge between the conscious and unconscious mind. Conscious breathing patterns can influence your energetic state, reduce stress, and activate healing.

Practice:

1.   Inhale for 4 counts, hold for 4, exhale for 6.

2.   As you breathe, imagine light flowing into your cells with each inhale and toxins being released with each exhale.

3.   Practice for 5–10 minutes daily or during moments of imbalance.

Why it works: Breath modulates heart rate, brainwave states, and the autonomic nervous system, creating coherence throughout the body's quantum systems.

Coherence Meditation (Heart-Brain Alignment)

Creating harmony between your heart and brain enhances emotional stability and bodily healing.

Practice:

1.   Place your hand on your heart and bring your focus to this area.

2.   Recall a moment of gratitude or love.

3.   Breathe slowly and feel the positive emotion expand through your body.

4.   Remain in this state for 5–15 minutes.

Why it works: Studies show that coherent heart rhythms influence brainwave activity, reducing cortisol and enhancing immune function.

Subconscious Reprogramming

Your subconscious stores emotional wounds and limiting beliefs that affect your body's energy field.

Practice:

1. Use affirmations or energy psychology tools like EFT to target core beliefs (e.g., "I am not safe", "I don't deserve to heal").

2. Repeat empowering statements such as: "I am whole. My body supports my well-being."

3. Visualize old beliefs being dissolved and replaced with light.

Why it works: The subconscious governs autonomic functions and healing responses. Reprogramming shifts your inner blueprint.

Energy Field Clearing

Stagnant or negative energy can accumulate in your field, affecting vitality.

Practice:

1. Use sound (singing bowls, humming, chanting) or movement (qigong, shaking, dance) to shift energy.

2. Visualize your body surrounded by light, pushing out dense or stuck energy.

3. Try a salt bath, smudging, or nature immersion to clear and reset.

Why it works: Your biofield interacts with your physical body. Keeping it clear enhances the flow of life force energy (Qi, Prana).

Conclusion: You Are the Healer

Quantum healing teaches us a fundamental truth: the mind and body are not separate, they are intertwined reflections of the same energetic field. Just as quantum particles respond to observation and intention, your body responds to your thoughts, emotions, and beliefs.

The practices in this chapter aren't just self-help tools, they are invitations to access the innate intelligence within you. Whether through meditation, visualization, breathwork, or emotional release, you are activating healing from within.

You are not at the mercy of diagnosis or circumstance. You are a conscious participant in your own well-being.

Remember:

1. Your thoughts influence your cells.

2. Your emotions carry a healing frequency.

3. Your attention directs the flow of life-force energy.

You are the quantum healer of your own life.

As we transition into the next chapter, we'll explore how to maintain this inner alignment across all areas of life. You'll learn how to build coherence between your heart, mind, environment, and relationships, so that healing becomes your natural state, not just a temporary breakthrough.

In Chapter 10, *Quantum Coherence: Building a Harmonious Life*, you'll discover how to sustain elevated energy and live in continuous resonance with your highest potential.

Chapter 10

Quantum Coherence: Building a Harmonious Life

10. Introduction: The Power of Inner Harmony

Have you ever felt like you're doing everything right, thinking positively, visualizing success, taking action, yet something still feels off? Like your mind is running ahead of your heart, your emotions are out of sync with your goals, or your daily actions aren't quite lining up with your deeper purpose? This is not failure, it's a lack of coherence.

Quantum coherence refers to the alignment of multiple elements in a unified and harmonious state. In physics, coherence allows quantum particles to function in perfect synchrony, amplifying their power. In human terms, coherence is when your thoughts, emotions, intentions, and actions all resonate on the same frequency, creating clarity, ease, and flow in your life.

When you operate in a state of coherence, you become a powerful conductor of energy. Your decisions feel more intuitive, your manifestations unfold more naturally, and your inner world reflects peace even in times of uncertainty. This chapter is about showing you how to access that state, not occasionally, but consistently.

We'll explore the science behind coherence, teach you how to align the layers of your consciousness, and guide you through a series of practical tools and reflections that help you live in resonance with your highest self. Because true power doesn't come from doing more, it comes from being aligned.

10.1.   Understanding Quantum Coherence

In quantum physics, coherence describes the state in which particles are in perfect sync with one another, vibrating at the same frequency, moving with shared purpose, and amplifying each other's influence. This coherence enables quantum systems to perform extraordinary tasks, like quantum computing, where information is processed exponentially faster due to this synchronized state.

Now, imagine applying this concept to your life.

Human coherence happens when your mind, emotions, body, and energy are aligned. It's when your thoughts don't contradict your emotions, your words reflect your values, and your actions align with your purpose. You've likely experienced moments of coherence: when you're fully present, your intuition is sharp, and everything seems to flow with ease. That's coherence in action.

Just as coherence in quantum systems increases their power, coherence in your inner world increases your effectiveness, presence, and influence. When you're in this state, you become more magnetic to opportunities, more attuned to your intuition, and more resilient in the face of challenges.

"When you are in coherence, your energy field becomes stronger, more organized, and more influential."

In the next section, we'll look at how to identify when you're in (or out of) coherence, and how to begin cultivating this powerful state on demand.

10.2. Aligning Mind, Body, and Energy: The Core of Coherence

Imagine a symphony where every instrument is playing a different tune. The result is chaos, disjointed, unpleasant, and uninspiring. But when every instrument aligns to a single composition, something magical happens: harmony. This is the essence of **quantum coherence**, a state where your thoughts, emotions, physical actions, and energy fields are in synchronized alignment, amplifying your ability to manifest and sustain success, health, and joy.

The Science Behind Coherence

In quantum physics, coherence describes particles vibrating in unison, producing a powerful, focused energy. Similarly, when all parts of your inner and outer world are attuned to a singular intention, you become energetically coherent, a powerful attractor for your desires.

The HeartMath Institute has demonstrated that emotional coherence, especially through elevated states like love, gratitude, and appreciation, affects not only heart rhythms but brain wave patterns and hormonal balance. In other words, coherence isn't just metaphysical, it's physiological.

Why Coherence Matters in Everyday Life

Disconnection shows up in everyday life when:

1. You set goals with your mind but doubt them in your heart.

2.   You say you want success but act from fear.

3.   You visualize abundance but speak words of lack.

These contradictions scramble your energetic signal, like trying to tune into a radio station while broadcasting static. But when your inner dialogue, emotions, and physical habits support a common vision, the universe responds with clarity.

Bringing the Systems Into Alignment

Here's how to foster coherence on multiple levels:

1.   **Mental Alignment:** Train your mind to focus on what you desire rather than what you fear. Use intentional thoughts and empowering beliefs.

2.   **Emotional Alignment:** Emotions are your vibrational messengers. Practice heart-based emotions like gratitude and joy to anchor your desired state.

3.   **Physical Alignment:** Your body stores patterns. Move it in ways that mirror confidence and strength. Good posture, exercise, and breathwork all send cues of harmony.

4.   **Energetic Alignment:** Use meditation, energy healing, or grounding techniques to clear blocks and recalibrate your frequency.

When all levels of your being are coherent, you become a clear channel for your intentions to flow into form.

10.3. Recognizing and Resolving Incoherence

Just as coherence empowers, **incoherence disempowers**. Recognizing when you're out of alignment is the first step to restoring harmony.

Signs of Incoherence:

1. Feeling scattered or mentally foggy

2. Emotional turbulence or mood swings

3. Self-sabotaging behaviors

4. Chronic fatigue or physical tension

5. Conflicting desires (e.g., wanting freedom but fearing change)

These are not failures, they are *feedback*. They're your inner systems signaling that something is out of sync.

The Roots of Incoherence

Most incoherence stems from:

1. **Unconscious beliefs**: Limiting stories from childhood or society.

2. **Emotional suppression**: Avoiding pain instead of processing it.

3. **Lifestyle mismatches**: Living routines that clash with your vision.

If you're holding a vision of success but living habits that reinforce struggle, the mismatch causes energetic resistance. You may attract opportunities, but lack the coherence to sustain or recognize them.

A Coherence Recalibration Process

Here's a simple, powerful practice to return to harmony:

1. **Pause and Scan** – Take a breath and ask, *"Where do I feel out of alignment?"* Notice the part of you that's resisting your vision.

2. **Name the Conflict** – Identify the disconnect. Maybe your body is tired, but your mind is pushing. Maybe your heart says yes, but your habits say no.

3. **Dialogue with the Disruption** – Ask this part of you, *"What do you need to feel safe aligning with my vision?"* Honor its wisdom.

4. **Breathe into Alignment** – Close your eyes and visualize all aspects of yourself syncing to a unified rhythm, mind, heart, body, and energy field.

5. **Choose a Coherent Action** – Take one small action that reflects the alignment you're calling in.

Coherence doesn't mean perfection, it means congruence. It's about living from a centered, unified truth.

10.4. The Role of the Heart in Creating Coherence

While the mind often takes center stage in personal development, the **heart** is the true conductor of coherence. In both ancient spiritual traditions and modern scientific studies, the heart is recognized not just as an organ, but as an intelligent center, emotional, intuitive, and energetically potent.

The Heart's Electromagnetic Power

The HeartMath Institute has revealed that the electromagnetic field generated by the heart is **60 times stronger** than that of the brain and can be measured several feet away from the body. This field acts as a broadcast system, transmitting your emotional and energetic state to the world, and even influencing others.

When you're in a state of **heart coherence**, cultivating emotions like love, compassion, gratitude, and peace, your nervous system, brain waves, and hormonal system fall into sync. This inner harmony not only boosts your health but **amplifies your manifesting power**.

Heart Coherence and Intuition

Have you ever had a "gut feeling" that turned out to be right? That intuitive nudge often originates in the heart. Studies show the heart senses changes in the environment seconds before the brain does. When your heart is coherent, your **intuition sharpens**, guiding you toward people, decisions, and actions aligned with your highest good.

Practices for Cultivating Heart Coherence

1. **Heart-Focused Breathing**

   Breathe slowly and deeply, directing your attention to the area around your heart.

Inhale for 5 seconds, exhale for 5 seconds.

2.   **Generate a Positive Emotion**

While breathing, recall a time you felt deep love, joy, or gratitude.

Feel that emotion expand in your chest and radiate outward.

3.   **Radiate and Broadcast**

Visualize that energy extending beyond your body, creating a ripple of coherence.

Even just **2 minutes** of this practice can shift your emotional baseline, elevate your frequency, and restore alignment between your heart and your higher purpose.

Tip: Begin your day with heart coherence. It calibrates your entire system for clarity, resilience, and aligned action.

10.5.   Daily Coherence Routines: Living in Flow

Lasting coherence isn't built through occasional practice, it's created through **consistent, conscious habits** that reinforce alignment. Think of coherence as a muscle that strengthens with use. The more you train it, the more naturally you live in a state of harmony.

A Coherent Day-in-the-Life

Here's how a day rooted in coherence might look:

1.   **Morning**: Begin with 5 minutes of heart coherence breathing. Set an intention for how you want to feel and act today.

2.   **Midday**: Take a brief awareness break. Check in: *Is my mind focused? Is my energy calm? Are my actions aligned?*

3.   **Evening**: Reflect through journaling. What felt aligned? What pulled you out of sync? What brought joy or tension?

4.   **Night**: Visualize your next day going smoothly, and feel gratitude for all that went well.

This rhythm creates a self-sustaining feedback loop of coherence, where awareness reinforces intention, and intention reinforces results.

Coherence Anchors for Daily Life

1.   **Music**: Create playlists that evoke calm, joy, or motivation. Sound frequencies can recalibrate your nervous system.

2.   **Movement**: Walks in nature, yoga, or intentional stretching restore body coherence.

3.   **Environment**: Surround yourself with visual cues, images, affirmations, or objects that reflect your vision of a harmonious life.

4.   **Language**: Speak words that affirm clarity, peace, and purpose. Self-talk is an energetic directive.

When your daily rituals are tuned to coherence, your life becomes a flowing expression of clarity, creativity, and abundance.

10.6.   Conclusion: A Life in Resonance

Imagine waking up each day not in chaos or confusion, but in clarity, balance, and peace. Imagine making decisions, not out of fear or urgency, but from a place of deep inner knowing. That's the power of quantum coherence: a life where your thoughts, emotions, intentions, and actions resonate in unison with your highest self.

This chapter has shown you that coherence is not merely a mystical state, it is a **trainable frequency**. It's the alignment between your **inner world and outer expression**, your **mind and body**, your **goals and emotions**, your **heart and vision**. And when you live in this state, the universe responds in kind. Opportunities become clearer. Challenges become invitations. Life becomes lighter and more meaningful.

The Coherent Self in Action

A coherent person:

1.   **Thinks clearly**, choosing empowering narratives.

2.   **Feels deeply**, yet responds rather than reacts.

3.   **Acts intentionally**, grounded in values and vision.

4.   **Creates effortlessly**, because their energy flows without internal conflict.

When coherence becomes your baseline, **success is no longer a struggle**. It becomes an extension of your state of being. Wealth, love, health, and fulfillment flow toward you, not because you chase them, but because you've become a resonant match.

Your Next Step

You don't need to master coherence overnight. Begin where you are. Practice small moments of alignment. Breathe with intention. Speak with clarity. Feel with honesty. Act with integrity.

Let these micro-practices build a macro reality, one of fulfillment, flow, and freedom.

"When you are in harmony with yourself, you are in harmony with the universe."

In the next chapter, we'll explore how this harmony across thoughts, feelings, and actions influences one of the most misunderstood forces in the quantum world, **time**. Prepare to discover how you can bend timelines, accelerate outcomes, and unlock higher-speed transformations through the mastery of your internal alignment.

Next Up: Chapter 11 , Quantum Timelines: Bending Time with Consciousness

Chapter 11

Quantum Timelines: Bending Time with Consciousness

11. Introduction: Time is Not What You Think

Have you ever noticed how time seems to slow down during a moment of awe, or how it races ahead when you're under stress? That's no coincidence. Our experience of time isn't fixed; it's fluid, subjective, and influenced by perception.

Now imagine this: You're walking through a train station. Around you are dozens of platforms, each representing a different destination, a different life. The train you board isn't determined by chance; it's chosen by the direction of your focus, your emotions, your beliefs. This is how quantum time works.

We've been taught to see time as a rigid line, past, present, future, unfolding in a single direction. But what if time is not linear? What if it's flexible, multidimensional, and even responsive to your consciousness?

Quantum physics reveals that time doesn't flow like an arrow; instead, it behaves like a field where all possibilities already exist. And if that's true, then your future isn't something you passively arrive at, it's something you can *intentionally* shape.

Think of your life like a series of parallel timelines, each representing a different version of who you could become. In one timeline, you play it safe. In another, you take a leap. In yet another, you're already living your dream. The secret to choosing the timeline you desire lies not in waiting, but in aligning your thoughts, emotions, and actions with it now.

This chapter is about collapsing the gap between where you are and where you want to be, by mastering time from a quantum perspective. You'll learn how to shift timelines, accelerate breakthroughs, and live as your future self *today*. Because time isn't just something you move through. It's something you *create with*.

11.1. Time, According to Quantum Physics

In classical physics, time is absolute. It's the ticking clock, the aging body, the sun rising and setting. But quantum physics paints a radically different picture, one where time can bend, stretch, and even disappear.

The Illusion of Linearity

In quantum mechanics, particles can exist in multiple states at once. They're not bound by a single trajectory until observed. This concept challenges our linear notion of time, suggesting that multiple futures may already exist, waiting to be activated by your focus and intention.

Physicist David Bohm spoke of the "implicate order", a deeper reality in which time and space are enfolded, not fixed. This implies that your past does not strictly determine your future. Instead, consciousness plays a pivotal role in shaping which future unfolds.

"The distinction between past, present, and future is only a stubbornly persistent illusion.", Albert Einstein

Time as a Field of Possibilities

Imagine time not as a line, but as a field, a vast landscape of parallel possibilities. Each choice, belief, and emotion you hold creates a ripple that nudges you toward one timeline or another.

Let's take a practical example. Think of a moment when you made a small choice, a last-minute event you decided to attend, or a conversation you nearly didn't have. That moment may have dramatically altered the course of your life. Now realize: those forks in the road are happening constantly. Each one opens a new track.

This is where quantum potential and personal transformation meet. You are not a prisoner of time, you are a participant in its unfolding. Your present awareness holds the power to influence both your future and your perception of the past.

The Role of the Observer

As we explored in earlier chapters, the observer effect in quantum physics tells us that observation changes outcome. In the context of time, this means that *how you observe your life*, your memories, your present situation, your vision for the future, literally alters the timeline you inhabit.

When you observe your future not as something distant but as something unfolding now, you activate new possibilities. You collapse the wave of potentiality into a single, empowered reality.

So how do you consciously select and shift into a new timeline? That's exactly what we'll explore next.

11.2. Collapsing Timelines: Choosing a New Reality

Imagine standing at a crossroads in your life. In front of you stretch countless paths, each leading to a different version of your future. Some are filled with struggle, others with joy, abundance, and growth. What determines which path you actually take? Not time. Not effort. But your alignment.

If every potential version of your future already exists in the quantum field, then a quantum leap doesn't require years of hustle, it requires coherence between who you are and what you desire.

Collapsing a timeline means intentionally shifting your internal state, your thoughts, emotions, and identity, to match the energetic frequency of a new outcome. When this alignment is sustained, your external world begins to rearrange to reflect your new trajectory.

This is where quantum theory becomes personal: you don't passively wait for change, you become the version of yourself who already has what you desire.

How to Collapse Timelines:

1. **Clarity** – Define the version of your future self you want to step into. Be vivid. Be specific. Imagine what they wear, how they think, the choices they make.

2. **Embodiment** – Act, speak, and feel as if you're already living that reality. This isn't pretending, it's practicing. Identity precedes outcome.

3. **Emotional Anchoring** – Sustain the emotional frequency of the desired timeline, joy, confidence, freedom, peace. These are not rewards; they're requirements.

4. **Observation and Gratitude** – Notice synchronicities. Celebrate even small shifts and treat them as signs of alignment. Gratitude amplifies the signal you send into the quantum field.

Case Study: Jairo Alonso, also known as Dr. Quantum, had struggled with adversity and financial challenges for years. After discovering quantum timeline techniques, he began acting as if he were already financially free, tracking his money like a CEO, affirming abundance, and upgrading his self-worth. His unwavering determination and entrepreneurial spirit led him to transform his life. Within a few months, he managed to turn his passion for trading into a solid and steady source of income, eventually becoming a successful entrepreneur and millionaire

He didn't "earn his way" out. He aligned his way out.

Integrated Timeline Collapsing Practice:

Ask yourself: *"What version of me already has what I desire?"* Then:

1. **Visualize Two Timelines** – Close your eyes and imagine two timelines side by side. One represents your current path. The other reflects your desired future. See both clearly and notice the energetic difference.

2. **Step Into the Desired Timeline** – In your mind's eye, physically and energetically shift into the new timeline. Breathe deeply and align your posture, tone, and internal dialogue with this new identity. Feel the shift.

3. **Anchor the Emotion** – Let yourself feel the emotional signature of this timeline, confidence, clarity, joy, relief. Hold it in your body. Smile. Say out loud: *"I choose this reality now."*

4. **Take One Affirming Action** – Do something immediately that reflects the version of you from

the new timeline. Make a bold decision, write the email, dress differently, speak with certainty.

5.   **Repeat Daily** – This isn't a one-time exercise. Repeat it daily to strengthen the signal and reinforce the shift. Each day, the reality you've chosen gets closer until it becomes your lived experience.

"When you begin living as your future self today, the quantum field responds by collapsing the timeline that matches your new identity."

Up next, we'll explore how your past may still be anchoring you to old timelines, and how to energetically release them to step fully into your chosen future.

11.3.   Releasing the Past: Untangling from Old Timelines

If collapsing a timeline is about stepping into your desired future, then releasing a timeline is about letting go of the past that no longer serves you.

Every belief, memory, or emotional wound that you carry acts like an anchor, keeping you tethered to an outdated version of yourself. These anchors prevent you from fully embodying your future identity, no matter how vividly you visualize it.

Quantum physics teaches us that the past is not fixed; it exists as a wave of potential, just like the future. By changing how you observe and relate to your past, you can shift its energetic influence and free yourself to move forward.

The Weight of Emotional Entanglement

Old timelines are often held in place by unresolved emotional energy, guilt, regret, anger, fear, shame. These emotions create feedback loops that keep you observing and reinforcing the same patterns.

Ask yourself:

1.   What part of my past do I keep replaying?

2.   What identity have I formed around this event?

3.   What belief did I adopt because of this experience?

Often, we don't realize we're still living from a version of ourselves that no longer exists, until we choose to observe it differently.

Quantum Release and Reintegration Practice

This guided release helps you energetically sever ties with outdated versions of you while reclaiming the wisdom they offer.

1.   **Identify the Anchor** – Bring to mind an event, belief, or relationship that feels heavy or limiting. See it clearly. Feel where it lives in your body.

2.   **Acknowledge Its Role** – Thank the memory or belief for the role it played. Even pain has purpose when it becomes a catalyst for growth.

3.   **Visualize the Cord** – Imagine a golden thread connecting you to that past version. Now, picture yourself gently holding the thread in your hand.

4.   **Cut and Reclaim** – Visualize yourself cutting the cord with a beam of light or a loving breath. As the

cord dissolves, see energy flowing back into your body, your power, your clarity, your freedom.

5. **Breathe into the Void** – Sit for a moment in stillness. Let your breath fill the space that was once held by the past. Affirm: *"I am no longer bound to who I was. I choose who I become."*

6. **Reintegrate the Wisdom** – Ask: *"What strength or insight can I carry forward from this timeline?"* Let it rise gently, and welcome it into your current self.

"Your past only defines you for as long as you keep identifying with it. You are not your history. You are your frequency."

Moving Beyond the Loop

When you release an old timeline, you're not erasing the memory, you're transforming your relationship with it. You no longer react from that place. You no longer define yourself by it. And most importantly, you stop creating your future from it.

This is how you reclaim your creative power. This is how you become a master of your timeline.

In the next section, we'll explore how your perception of time itself, linear vs. nonlinear, affects your ability to manifest change rapidly and sustainably.

11.4. Time Perception and Timeline Shifts

We often speak of time as if it moves in a straight line, past, present, future. But quantum physics tells a different story. Time, in the quantum sense, is not fixed or linear. It is fluid, responsive, and subjective, shaped by your focus and frequency.

This means your perception of time isn't just a mental concept, it is a powerful tool that can either limit or accelerate your transformation.

The Illusion of Linear Time

Most people live according to "chronological time":

1.   I was there.

2.   Now I'm here.

3.   One day I'll be there.

But in quantum reality, all potential timelines already exist. The version of you who has already achieved your goal is not in some distant future. That version exists now, as a vibrational reality waiting for you to match it.

When you collapse the illusion of linearity, you open the door to nonlinear leaps. Healing that "should have" taken years can happen in moments. Shifts that felt far away become accessible now.

"Time is not the cause of transformation, alignment is."

Time Expansion vs. Time Contraction

Your inner state determines how you experience time:

1.   **Fear contracts time.** When you're anxious, overwhelmed, or rushed, time feels like it's slipping away. You operate from survival mode.

2. **Presence expands time.** When you're calm, focused, and aligned, time feels spacious. You move with clarity and efficiency.

By learning to shift your perception of time, you can consciously accelerate the arrival of your desired outcomes.

Timeline Expansion Practice

Use this practice to rewire how your body and mind experience time:

1. **Enter Stillness** – Close your eyes and take three deep breaths. Let go of urgency. Let go of "how long it should take."

2. **Visualize Timeless Success** – Imagine your goal already fulfilled. Notice that time doesn't exist in this vision, only presence, confidence, and certainty.

3. **Recalibrate Your Pace** – Affirm: *"There is no rush. I am exactly where I need to be. My success is inevitable."*

4. **Move from Alignment, Not Pressure** – Let inspired actions arise naturally. Trust that your timing is perfect.

"Presence is the portal through which quantum timelines become accessible."

In the next section, we'll explore how synchronicity reveals you're on the right timeline, and how to follow the signs with clarity and trust.

11.5. Following the Signs: Synchronicity and Timeline Navigation

As you begin shifting timelines and stepping into new versions of yourself, something magical happens: the universe responds. Not with loud announcements, but with subtle winks, signs, synchronicities, nudges.

Synchronicity is the language of the quantum field. It's how life lets you know: *you're in alignment.*

What Is Synchronicity?

Synchronicity is a meaningful coincidence with no logical explanation, yet perfect timing. It's when you think of someone and they call. When a book falls off a shelf with the exact message you needed. When an unexpected opportunity matches your next-level vision.

These moments are not accidents. They are reflections of your energetic alignment.

"When the inner world shifts, the outer world starts to mirror it."

Navigating with Trust

Synchronicities are like trail markers on a hike, you don't need to see the entire path to know you're headed in the right direction. You just need to keep moving from one sign to the next.

Start asking:

1. What signs have been showing up lately?

2. What is life trying to tell me?

3. What decision feels most aligned, even if it's not logical?

The more you trust these nudges, the more frequent and obvious they become.

Daily Quantum Navigation Practice

Build your intuitive muscle and learn to read the signs:

1. **Morning Intention** – Ask: *"What do I need to notice today to stay aligned with my highest timeline?"* Then stay open.

2. **Track the Magic** – Keep a small synchronicity journal. Log signs, patterns, nudges, and gut feelings.

3. **Follow the Energy** – Make at least one decision daily based on intuition rather than logic alone. Notice how things unfold.

4. **Acknowledge Alignment** – Every time something "just works out," celebrate it. Gratitude amplifies the signal.

Synchronicity is not just a feel-good phenomenon, it is functional. It helps you navigate uncertainty with ease, reminding you that you are not alone. You are part of a quantum intelligence that responds to your frequency.

In the next section, we'll integrate everything we've explored and show you how to become a conscious time traveler, shaping your life moment by moment with clarity, trust, and power.

11.6. Quantum Timewalking: Living as Your Future Self Now

If you could meet your future self, the one who has already created the life you desire, what would they tell you? What would they *feel* like? How would they act, walk, speak, and make decisions?

In quantum reality, this future version of you already exists. Your role is not to chase that version, but to *embody* it now. This is the essence of quantum timewalking: becoming the version of yourself who already has what you want, and making choices from that identity today.

"You don't wait to become your future self. You remember who you are, and return to it."

The Science Behind Identity-Based Shifting

Your brain doesn't distinguish between vividly imagined experiences and real ones. Neuroscience confirms that rehearsing a new identity, through thought, feeling, and behavior, literally rewires your brain and nervous system.

Quantum physics teaches us that the field responds to frequency, not effort. So when you align your thoughts, emotions, and actions with the reality you *choose*, you shift timelines.

This is not about faking it. It's about *tuning in* to the energy of your future self until it feels familiar.

Future Self Embodiment Practice

1. **Close the Gap** – Visualize your future self clearly. What do they look like? How do they carry themselves? What do they *know* to be true?

2. **Feel It Fully** – Embody the emotions of already having what you desire, confidence, peace, joy, abundance.

3. **Ask Before Action** – When facing a choice, pause and ask: *"What would my future self do here?"* Let that version guide you.

4. **Make It Daily** – The more often you align with your future self, the faster your current reality shifts to match it.

"Timelines don't shift by chance. They shift by identity."

When you walk as your future self, you collapse time and become the bridge between what was and what will be.

Conclusion: Time Is Your Canvas

You are not bound by a linear clock. You are a multidimensional being with access to infinite timelines, each carrying a different version of your potential.

Throughout this chapter, you've learned that time is flexible. Your consciousness, not circumstance, determines the pace, shape, and trajectory of your life. Whether through collapsing limiting timelines, shifting perception, following synchronicity, or embodying your future self, you hold the power to transform time into your creative ally.

"Time does not hold you. You hold time."

So, what timeline will you choose now? Will you wait for change, or *become* the change?

Your next moment holds the power to alter your entire trajectory. Step into it deliberately.

In the next chapter, we'll explore how to create lasting transformation by taking bold, quantum leaps into the life you've only imagined, until now.

Reflection Prompts

    1.   What is one belief about time I'm ready to release?

    2.   What signs has the universe shown me recently?

    3.   What action would my future self take today?

Write your responses. Let them guide your next leap.

Chapter 12

Quantum Leap: Transforming Your Life with Bold Change

12. Introduction: The Science and Spirit of Sudden Shifts

Carla stared at the email. A job offer from a company she had once dreamt of working for. But something inside her said no. The next day, she turned it down, packed a suitcase, and flew to Bali to start the wellness retreat she'd secretly mapped out in her journal. One bold decision, and her life was never the same.

These moments aren't just dramatic, they're quantum. They reflect the same principle observed in quantum physics: the quantum jump. In this phenomenon, a particle suddenly leaps from one state to another without passing through the in-between. It doesn't inch forward, it leaps.

What if transformation in your life could work the same way?

A quantum leap isn't about striving harder. It's about aligning with a new level of being and letting go of the limitations that kept you stuck. It's when clarity replaces confusion, confidence replaces fear, and massive progress replaces slow steps.

In this chapter, you'll learn how to identify the signs that you're ready for a leap, prepare your mindset, and take action that accelerates change in every area of life. Whether you're looking for a breakthrough in your career, relationships, finances, or purpose, the principles here will guide you toward your next big shift.

Big Idea: Just like in quantum physics, transformation in life doesn't have to be incremental. It can be instantaneous, when you shift your frequency, identity, and intention all at once.

12.1.   What Is a Quantum Leap?

In traditional growth models, we're taught to progress step by step. But quantum leaps defy linear logic. They involve a sudden, often dramatic, change in circumstance or consciousness that can catapult you into a new level of reality.

In quantum physics, a quantum leap (or quantum jump) is when an electron absorbs energy and instantaneously moves to a higher energy orbit. It doesn't climb gradually, it just appears in the new state. Likewise, in life, a quantum leap happens when:

1.   A limiting belief is shattered.

2.   A powerful decision is made.

3.   A new level of identity is embraced.

You don't need to wait for years of incremental change. A new reality becomes available the moment you align with it internally.

Examples of Quantum Leaps in Life:

1.   Leaving a secure job to start your own business, and succeeding rapidly.

2.   Ending a long-standing pattern of unhealthy relationships and finding true love.

3.   Moving from financial struggle to unexpected abundance after a mindset shift.

These leaps may look sudden on the outside, but they are often the result of internal alignment, courage, and clarity.

Mini Reflection: Ask yourself: "If I wasn't afraid, what leap would I take today?"

Quantum Shift Reminder: The leap isn't about *getting there*. It's about *becoming* the person who already is there. Once your inner reality shifts, your outer world will follow.

New Perspective: You're not required to climb every step of the ladder. Some steps can be skipped entirely, when your frequency upgrades, your reality shifts to match.

12.2. The Energy Behind the Leap: Why Bold Change Happens

Before a quantum leap happens, there's often a buildup of inner tension, the kind that comes from knowing you're meant for more but feeling stuck in place. This inner pressure creates potential energy that, when released, can propel you into a new state of being.

The Key Drivers of a Quantum Leap:

1. **Emotional Intensity:** Strong emotions, whether excitement or frustration, signal readiness for change. They disrupt inertia and fuel bold decisions.

2. **Vision Clarity:** The clearer your vision, the easier it is to leap. When you see your desired outcome vividly, your mind and energy begin aligning with it.

3. **Energetic Alignment:** When your thoughts, emotions, and actions are in harmony with your vision, you build the momentum needed to leap.

4. **Identity Expansion:** Leaps occur when you let go of who you've been and embody a more empowered version of yourself.

5. **Spiritual Readiness:** Sometimes, the leap is a calling from your higher self, a whisper that says, "It's time."

Insight: Your biggest quantum leaps often follow your greatest discomfort. That discomfort is not punishment, it's preparation.

Quantum Insight: Just as a particle leaps without traversing the space in between, your leap doesn't require a linear route. It requires resonance, matching the frequency of the life you desire.

Quick Timeline Collapsing Exercise:

1. Close your eyes and visualize your desired reality already existing.

2. Feel the emotions associated with it: joy, freedom, peace, excitement.

3. Now ask yourself: "What belief or behavior am I still holding onto that belongs to the *old* version of me?"

4. Take a deep breath and say out loud: "I collapse the timeline of waiting. I step into alignment with my new reality now."

5. Open your eyes and write one bold action you can take today from this new identity.

12.3.   Signs You're Ready for a Quantum Leap

Sometimes we wait for external confirmation that it's time to make a move, but your inner world will often show the signs long before your outer world does.

Indicators You're on the Edge of a Leap:

1.   **Persistent Restlessness:** You feel agitated with your current circumstances, even if they're "fine." This unrest is your soul's nudge toward growth.

2.   **Sudden Downloads or Clarity:** You experience flashes of insight or an inner knowing that there's something bigger waiting for you.

3.   **Increased Synchronicity:** You keep encountering people, messages, or opportunities that align with your deeper desires.

4.   **Emotional Rollercoaster:** One moment you're excited, the next you're anxious. These emotional swings often signal energetic recalibration.

5.   **Loss of Interest in the Old:** What used to satisfy or distract you now feels dull or irrelevant. Your old self is losing grip.

6.   **Desire for Radical Change:** You're not interested in tweaking your current life, you crave transformation.

Inner Prompt: Think of a time you experienced a deep inner knowing that it was time for change. What did it feel like? What nudges are showing up for you now?

12.4. Aligning with the Leap: Preparing Your Mind and Energy

To make a quantum leap, you must first become an energetic match for the new reality. This isn't about faking it until you make it, it's about genuinely embodying the version of you who already lives that reality.

Steps to Align with Your Quantum Leap:

1. **Decide with Finality:** Half-hearted decisions won't create leaps. Declare what you want, and own it completely.

2. **Anchor Your Identity:** Ask: Who is the version of me living that reality? Then start thinking, speaking, and behaving like them now.

3. **Elevate Your Environment:** Surround yourself with people, places, and content that reflect the energy of your new reality.

4. **Clear Resistance:** Use journaling, meditation, or coaching to identify and release fears, doubts, and limiting beliefs.

5. **Visualize Daily:** Vividly see yourself already living in your quantum leap. Feel the emotions and outcomes as real now.

6. **Take Inspired Action:** Action is the bridge between energy and manifestation. Do something bold that your future self would do.

Feel It Now: Hear the sounds, see the scenes, and sense the energy of your new reality. Smell the air, taste the victory. Make the leap real in your imagination, your subconscious won't know the difference.

Affirmation Upgrade: "I am not becoming, I already am. I walk boldly in the reality I've chosen."

Leap Readiness Tip: Write a letter from your future self describing how your life transformed after you took the leap. Read it every morning to condition your mind to expect that reality.

12.5.   The 7-Day Leap Challenge

Transformation requires momentum. This challenge is designed to train your nervous system for courage, build energetic consistency, and activate synchronicity.

For the Next 7 Days:

Morning Focus: Each morning, ask: "What bold move would the future me make today?"

Bold Action: Take one aligned action, big or small, that reflects the energy of your new self.

Evening Reflection: Keep a Leap Journal. At the end of each day, reflect:

1.   What did I do today that felt bold?

2.   What resistance did I overcome?

3.   What synchronicities, insights, or progress did I notice?

Example Journal Entry (Day 3): "I reached out to the client I've been too scared to pitch. They said yes to a meeting! I feel braver than I did yesterday."

Neurohack: After each bold move, close your eyes and take 20 seconds to feel successful, safe, and proud. This wires your nervous system to associate boldness with reward rather than risk.

Encouragement: Leaps don't need to be flashy. Sometimes the boldest act is having a tough conversation, setting a boundary, or finally saying yes to yourself.

This challenge builds confidence, rewires your brain for boldness, and accelerates your leap into the reality you were meant for.

12.6.   Conclusion: Leap, and the Net Will Appear

Quantum leaps don't follow logic. They follow alignment. They are the result of inner congruence, when your belief, energy, identity, and decision-making come into harmony with the version of life you desire.

The most powerful leaps are not those taken blindly, but those taken boldly, with eyes open, heart engaged, and spirit aligned.

You don't need to know every step in advance. The quantum field doesn't require a mapped route. It requires resonance. When your inner state matches your desired outcome, the universe responds.

Mirror Moment: What is the boldest version of you calling out for expression? What dream or decision have you delayed because it defies logic? What if now is the moment to say yes?

Leap Framework Recap:

1. **See it:** Visualize the reality you're ready for.

2. **Feel it:** Embody the emotional frequency of that reality.

3. **Align with it:** Make decisions and take actions from that new identity.

4. **Leap into it:** Move, speak, and show up as if it's already done.

Final Reflection: What would change if you trusted that bold action, taken from alignment, bends reality in your favor? What new timeline might open if you decided to leap now?

The truth is this: the net doesn't appear before you jump. It appears **because** you jumped.

This is your moment.

Say yes.

And leap.

Coming Up Next:

In the next chapter, we'll explore one of the most fascinating frontiers of quantum thinking, the concept of the *Multiverse*. You'll discover how parallel realities and infinite timelines may not just be science fiction, but a powerful lens for choosing and stepping into new versions of your life. Get ready to explore the infinite possibilities that exist beyond your current reality.

Chapter 13

The Multiverse: Exploring Infinite Possibilities

13. Introduction: Stepping Beyond the Horizon of Reality

Imagine waking up one morning and realizing that every choice you didn't make, every dream you put on hold, and every version of "what if" still exists, somewhere. In the vastness of the cosmos, quantum physics suggests that you're not limited to a single reality, but instead exist within a multiverse: a boundless web of parallel realities where countless versions of you are living out different experiences, shaped by different choices.

This chapter invites you to explore not only the science of the multiverse, but also the transformational power it holds for your personal growth. More than a theory, the multiverse becomes a lens through which you can expand your thinking, challenge your limitations, and awaken to the vast potential within you.

At the intersection of quantum mechanics and metaphysical wisdom lies a liberating truth: You are not stuck. You are not behind. You are not out of options. There are infinite paths ahead, and you get to choose.

Through this chapter, you'll learn how to:

1. Understand the multiverse from both a scientific and spiritual lens.

2. Shift from a single-track mindset to multidimensional awareness.

3. Access your highest timelines by aligning thought, emotion, and action.

4. Step into the version of you who already lives the life you desire.

As we begin, remember: You are not here to play small in one life. You are here to awaken to your multiversal nature, and to choose, with clarity and courage, the version of reality that empowers your highest self.

13.1. The Science and Spirituality of the Multiverse

The concept of a multiverse, once confined to science fiction, is now an active area of study in quantum mechanics, cosmology, and consciousness research. But long before scientists explored parallel realities, mystics, philosophers, and spiritual traditions spoke of simultaneous worlds, overlapping timelines, and infinite potential.

Quantum Theory Meets Infinite Possibility

In quantum mechanics, the "Many-Worlds Interpretation" suggests that all possible outcomes of a quantum event do in fact occur, each in its own distinct, parallel universe. Every decision you make, every action you take (or don't take), branches reality like a tree. There isn't just one path, you are coexisting with countless alternatives.

If this sounds abstract, think of it this way:

1. Every time you chose courage instead of fear, you created a new path.

2. Every time you turned left instead of right, a new timeline opened.

3. And every time you dared to dream bigger, a version of you began living that dream somewhere in the multiverse.

Spiritual Parallels

Spiritual teachings echo these ideas in other forms:

1. The belief that your soul is multidimensional.

2. That we exist in layers of reality beyond what the senses perceive.

3. That intuition, déjà vu, and synchronicity are glimpses into alternate timelines.

When science and spirit meet, they tell the same story: Reality is not fixed, it is fluid, expansive, and profoundly influenced by your consciousness.

Thought Prompt: What if your greatest dream isn't something you have to create from scratch, but something you simply need to align with?

In the sections ahead, we'll go deeper into how you can consciously navigate the multiverse, not with a spaceship, but with intention, energy, and choice.

13.2. Choosing Your Timeline: The Power of Conscious Alignment

If the multiverse holds infinite versions of your life, then which one are you living in right now? The answer lies in your alignment, your thoughts, emotions, and beliefs act as tuning forks, drawing you into the version of reality that matches your internal frequency.

The Law of Resonance

In both science and metaphysics, like attracts like. This principle is often described as the Law of Resonance. You don't get what you want, you get what you are in vibrational alignment with.

Want to shift to a reality where your dreams are already unfolding? Start by becoming energetically compatible with that version of life. Think the thoughts that version of you would think. Feel the feelings. Speak the words. Take the bold actions.

Just like tuning into a specific frequency on a radio, alignment tunes you into a specific timeline in the multiverse. And once you're tuned in, synchronicities accelerate, obstacles dissolve, and what once seemed far away begins showing up in real time.

Exercise: Timeline Alignment Visualization

1. Close your eyes and imagine the version of you already living your dream life.

2. What do they believe about themselves?

3. What do they do each day? Who are they surrounded by?

4. Now, embody that version of you, breathe as they would, speak as they would.

5. Ask: What is one action I can take today to anchor into this timeline?

13.3. Shifting Realities: Micro-Leaps and Identity Updates

Many people expect transformation to be dramatic, but most shifts begin subtly. Quantum shifts often start as micro-leaps: small changes in belief, behavior, or identity that create ripple effects through your reality.

Identity as the Portal

Your identity isn't fixed, it's a construct shaped by memory, perception, and repetition. When you update your identity, you shift the timelines available to you.

For example:

> The identity of "I'm a struggling artist" leads to different opportunities than "I'm a thriving creator."

> "I'm terrible with money" exists in a different timeline than "I am financially empowered."

Changing your identity is less about pretending and more about remembering, remembering who you truly are beneath the conditioning and limitations.

Micro-Leaps that Shift Timelines

Here are simple yet powerful micro-leaps:

1. Speak one empowering belief aloud each morning.

2. Introduce yourself in alignment with your future self ("I'm building a wellness brand," vs. "I'm trying to start a side hustle").

3.   Say yes to one aligned opportunity you'd normally avoid.

4.   Say no to something that no longer serves you.

Each micro-leap you take signals to the multiverse: "I'm ready to upgrade." And when the signal is clear, the shift is inevitable.

Thought Prompt: What part of your identity are you ready to release, and what timeline will that unlock?

13.4.   Navigating Quantum Choices: Decision as a Dimensional Tool

In the multiverse, each choice you make creates a branching pathway. What may seem like a small decision, a conversation, a new habit, or a different belief, has the power to shift you into an entirely new timeline.

Every Choice is a Portal

Every decision holds quantum weight. By choosing courage over fear, love over limitation, or growth over comfort, you open portals to higher outcomes.

From the perspective of quantum theory, all potential outcomes already exist. Your consciousness, through observation and intention, collapses one possibility into reality. When you hesitate to decide, you remain entangled in multiple potentials. But when you choose boldly, you activate a specific quantum thread.

The Power of Decisive Energy

Think of a quantum leap not as a magical event but as the consequence of sustained, intentional decisions.

Try this reflection:

1.   What are three choices I've been avoiding?

2.   What would my higher self decide?

3.   What's one bold decision I can make today that aligns with the timeline I want?

Quantum Navigation Tip: Choose from the version of you already living the life you desire. Let that version guide your next steps.

13.5.   Parallel Selves and Quantum Guidance

If the multiverse contains infinite versions of you, what can those other versions teach you?

Meeting Your Parallel Self

In meditation, visualization, or dreams, it is possible to connect with your parallel self, the one who already made the leap, took the risk, or healed completely. This version exists as a vibrational template. You can receive insight, energy, and guidance from them.

Practice: Parallel Self Dialogue

1.   Enter a relaxed state through deep breathing or meditation.

2.   Visualize a version of you who has already achieved the outcome you desire.

3.   Ask: What did you let go of? What habits or beliefs did you adopt? What do I need to know right now?

4.   Listen, feel, or intuit the response.

Document the experience. The more you connect with this self, the more you embody their energy.

The Science of Inner Knowing

While mainstream science doesn't yet fully embrace parallel self-dialogue, quantum theory allows for entangled information across space and time. Your subconscious may be tapping into these timelines more often than you realize, through intuition, gut feelings, or dreams.

Reflection Prompt: If your parallel self could speak to you daily, what would they remind you of?

In the next section, we'll bring together all these threads and learn how to intentionally surf multiversal possibilities, not just imagine them, but live them boldly.

13.6.   Surfing the Multiverse: How to Consciously Shift Timelines

The beauty of the multiverse isn't just in imagining endless possibilities, it's in realizing you can intentionally choose which one to live.

Your Thoughts Are the Steering Wheel

Your dominant thoughts and emotions act as vibrational coordinates that determine the timeline you're experiencing. When you dwell in fear, guilt, or limitation, you align with timelines where struggle persists. But when you consistently hold thoughts of freedom, expansion, and purpose, you resonate with realities where those qualities flourish.

Exercise: Timeline Calibration

1. Identify a current situation where you feel stuck.

2. Ask: What's the emotional frequency of my current response (e.g., fear, doubt)?

3. Then ask: What frequency would the version of me who has already overcome this operate from (e.g., courage, clarity)?

4. Each day, choose one action, thought, or belief that aligns with that elevated frequency.

This isn't about perfection, it's about tuning your internal state like a radio until you resonate with the signal of your desired reality.

Surfing Between Possibilities

Sometimes shifts are subtle. You wake up and feel a little clearer. A coincidence happens. A new idea sparks. These are signs you've stepped into a slightly different timeline. Over time, those small shifts compound into massive transformation.

The more deliberately you practice timeline surfing, the more fluid life becomes. You no longer feel confined by your past. You become the conscious navigator of infinite possibility.

Final Practice: Morning Multiverse Tune-In Each morning, ask:

1. What timeline am I choosing today?

2. How does this version of me think, feel, and act?

3. What one shift can I make to align with it now?

Then, live your day as if that version is already real. Because in the multiverse, it is.

Conclusion: Living as a Multiversal Being

You are not bound to a single path or outcome. The multiverse reveals that infinite versions of you already exist, each shaped by your choices, energy, and belief. Your power lies in choosing the reality that most aligns with your soul's vision.

This chapter has shown you how to:

1. Recognize the multiverse not as science fiction but as a reflection of quantum possibility.

2. Shift timelines through conscious decisions and emotional alignment.

3. Access guidance from parallel versions of yourself who already embody the life you desire.

You are not waiting for a better future, you are creating it by the frequency you hold and the focus you choose. Every moment is an invitation to leap into the timeline that reflects your highest truth.

You're not just imagining infinite possibilities. You're learning to live them.

Welcome to your multiversal life!

Chapter 14 (Bonus)

Quantum Identity Shifting: Becoming the Version of You Who Has Already Arrived

14. Introduction: The Self as a Field of Possibility

Brandon Stanton once thought of himself as someone who always played it safe, a dependable employee, a creature of habit. But after losing his job as a bond trader in Chicago in 2010, something shifted. He decided to move to New York City with little money and possessions to pursue a new hobby: photography. His initial goal was to photograph 10,000 people on the streets of New York and plot their pictures on a map. This project, Humans of New York, became massively popular and transformed his life.

Who are you, really? Are you the collection of your past memories, habits, and roles? Or are you a dynamic field of potential, capable of adopting new identities that align with your highest future?

In classical psychology, identity is seen as something relatively fixed, your personality, shaped by upbringing and past experiences. But in the quantum model, identity is fluid. The self is not a static point; it is a wave of potential realities. Who you are is who you observe yourself to be.

This chapter explores the powerful principle of identity shifting through the lens of quantum physics, Law of Attraction teachings, and the psychology of transformation. You'll learn how to collapse timelines by consciously becoming the version of you who already lives the life you desire.

14.1.   Understanding the Quantum Self

In quantum mechanics, particles exist in a state of superposition, holding multiple possibilities simultaneously, until observed. You, too, exist in superposition, capable of stepping into different versions of yourself based on observation, belief, and intention.

Your identity is not your name, your job, or even your personality. It is the energetic pattern you emit based on your beliefs, self-image, and expectations. The quantum self is not bound by the past. It is malleable, adaptable, and responsive to conscious focus.

"Change your concept of yourself and you will automatically change the world in which you live.", Neville Goddard

Key Insight:

You don't attract what you want. You attract who you are. Therefore, to experience a new reality, you must become a new version of yourself.

14.2.   The Physics of Identity Collapse

In quantum theory, a wave function represents all potential states. When an observer looks at the particle, the wave collapses into one outcome.

Likewise, your self-concept is a wave of potential identities. Every time you observe yourself through a new lens, "I am confident," "I am wealthy," "I am loved", you collapse your energetic field into a new experience of being. The universe responds not to your desires but to your dominant identity signature.

This collapse is not just philosophical, it's deeply practical. Your decisions, habits, body language, and emotional tone all stem from your identity. Shift the identity, and your reality follows.

"To change your reality, you must change the observer, that is, the version of you doing the observing.", Inspired by Quantum Theory

Reflection Prompt:

1. What identity have I unconsciously been observing myself as?

2. What new identity do I choose to embody today?

14.3.   The Self-Concept Equation

Your current identity is shaped by three forces:

1. **Memory** – Past experiences you identify with.

2. **Emotion** – The emotional tone you live in.

3. **Repetition** – The thoughts and behaviors you reinforce daily.

To shift identity:

1. **Revise memory**: Reinterpret past events to support a new narrative. Instead of "That failure proved I'm not good enough," choose "That failure prepared me to succeed."

2. **Elevate emotion**: Feel the feelings of the new version of you. Joy, certainty, confidence, choose them daily.

3.   **Rehearse repetition**: Visualize the new you, speak affirmations aloud, and take actions aligned with this version.

"You can't wait for a new reality to feel like a new person. You must feel like a new person to create a new reality.", Dr. Joe Dispenza

Daily Identity Reinforcement Practice:

1.   Morning Journal Prompt: "Today, I am showing up as the version of me who is _____."

2.   Affirm aloud: "I am becoming [insert identity], and every action I take confirms it."

3.   End-of-day reflection: "How did I embody my chosen identity today?"

Repeat for 21 days to reprogram your neural pathways and build consistency with your desired identity.

14.4.   The Quantum Mirror: Life Reflects Identity

The world you experience is a direct reflection of your internal identity. If you see yourself as unworthy, life mirrors that belief through rejection, lack, or stagnation. If you see yourself as powerful and abundant, life rises to meet that vision.

This isn't spiritual fluff, it's resonance. Your identity emits a frequency, and the quantum field reflects experiences that match that frequency. The moment you embody a new identity, your external world begins rearranging itself to reflect that inner shift.

"Life doesn't give you what you want. It gives you who you are.",
Neville Goddard

Daily Identity Alignment Practice Each morning, ask:

1. Who am I being today?

2. What thoughts, feelings, and actions define that version of me?

Then move through the day from that state, not as an effort, but as a natural alignment.

Add Journaling Reflection: In the evening, journal:

1. What showed up today that matched my chosen identity?

2. Where did I default to an old version of myself?

3. What will I embody more clearly tomorrow?

This consistent reflection helps track progress and reinforce intentional identity.

14.5. Identity Shift Activation

This guided exercise helps you embody and stabilize your quantum identity.

Quantum Identity Embodiment Practice (10 Minutes Daily):

1. Close your eyes and take deep, grounding breaths.

2.   Visualize the version of you who has already achieved your desired reality.

3.   Observe their posture, energy, voice, and expression.

4.   Step into their perspective. Become them now.

5.   Speak aloud: "I am [insert identity]. This is who I am now."

6.   Anchor the feeling in your body with a gesture, such as placing your hand on your heart.

Bonus Journal Prompt:

"As the version of me who is already [insert identity], today I will..."

Repeat for 21 days to rewire your subconscious mind and form a new energetic baseline.

This practice is not about pretending, it's about pre-living. When you live as your future self now, you collapse time and magnetize new outcomes faster.

14.6.   Conclusion: Choose Yourself Into Being

You are not a fixed entity. You are a dynamic field of potential identities, each waiting to be activated by your conscious choice. Quantum identity shifting isn't about becoming someone else, it's about becoming more of who you truly are.

Every thought, emotion, and action is a vote for the version of you you're embodying. If you want a new life, you must start living it from the inside out.

"You must assume the feeling of the wish fulfilled.", Neville Goddard

This is not wishful thinking, it's deliberate creation. Choose yourself into being.

Final   **Reflection:**
What version of yourself is already living the life you desire? What small action can you take today to live from that identity?

Your future self already exists. The moment you decide to become them, reality begins to shift.

In the next chapter, we'll zoom back out to explore how to harmonize all of your quantum potentials into one aligned, coherent life. You've learned to shift into the version of you who has arrived, now it's time to integrate and live fully as that self.

Chapter 15 (Bonus)

The Quantum Life Blueprint: Living as the Architect of Your Reality

15. Introduction: From Insight to Embodiment

Throughout this book, you've explored the profound mechanics of the quantum universe, from the Observer Effect to Superposition, Entanglement, and Quantum Leaps. You now understand that your thoughts, beliefs, emotions, and intentions are not just ephemeral inner states, they are real forces that shape the quantum field and influence the trajectory of your life.

But understanding is only the beginning. Transformation happens when knowledge becomes lifestyle.

This bonus chapter is your bridge from inspiration to integration. It distills the entire book into an actionable blueprint, a living, breathing framework for embodying quantum principles in your everyday life. Whether you're new to this journey or seeking a practical map to go deeper, what follows is designed to help you move from conscious creator to masterful architect of your reality.

Let this chapter be your daily compass, your go-to reference, and your activation manual.

15.1. The Quantum Life Formula: 7 Core Pillars of Embodied Creation

To live a quantum life is to live intentionally, energetically aligned, and boldly expansive. The following seven pillars synthesize the quantum principles explored throughout the book into a clear framework you can return to every day.

Quantum Clarity (Chapter 1 & 2)

Know what you want. Clarity of thought and desire is the gateway to manifestation. Your mind must project a coherent signal to the field. Vague intentions produce vague outcomes.

> **Practice:** Write out your top 3 life intentions every week. Ask, "What do I *really* want?"

Creative Superposition (Chapter 3)

Hold multiple possibilities. The universe responds to your dominant state, but that doesn't mean limiting yourself to one path. Stay open. The most aligned outcome may surprise you.

> **Practice:** Visualize three empowering outcomes. Feel into each one. Let your energy settle into the one that feels most expansive.

Conscious Observation (Chapter 4)

Where focus goes, energy flows. Your observation is not neutral. What you consistently attend to with emotion becomes your lived experience.

> **Practice:** Use daily mindfulness check-ins. Observe without judgment. Redirect to what you choose to grow.

Vibrational Alignment (Chapter 5 & 10)

Embody the frequency of your future. You don't manifest what you want. You manifest what you *are*. Your emotional and energetic state is the signal the universe echoes.

> **Practice:** Choose your state each morning. Use music, movement, or breathwork to elevate your frequency.

Quantum Relationships (Chapter 6 & 8)

Connect with resonance. You are entangled with others. Relationships either amplify or distort your signal. Choose resonance.

> **Practice:** Surround yourself with people who reflect your future, not your past. Cultivate collaborative coherence.

Identity Shifting (Chapter 11 & 14)

Become the version of you who has already arrived. Your identity is your operating system. Shift the self, and the world around you shifts in response.

> **Practice:** Every morning, ask: "Who am I being today?" Dress, walk, and speak as that version of you.

Quantum Action (Chapter 7, 9, 12)

Take bold, inspired steps. The field responds to movement. Action is the bridge between energy and matter.

> **Practice:** Each day, take one action your future self would take. No matter how small, let it be bold.

These seven principles form the architecture of quantum living. They are not rules, but frequencies. Not prescriptions, but portals.

In the next section, you'll discover how to apply them in a 30-day framework that transforms your energy, behavior, and outcomes, one intentional day at a time.

15.2.   The 30-Day Quantum Life Activation Framework

You don't become a new version of yourself overnight, but with daily quantum alignment, you shift realities faster than linear effort ever could. The following 30-day framework is a strategic immersion into quantum living.

Each week activates one of the core principles, layering depth and momentum as you go.

Week 1: Clarity & Observation, Choose Your Reality

1.   **Day 1:** Define your top 3 life intentions. Get crystal clear.

2.   **Day 2:** Observe your thoughts throughout the day. What's in alignment? What isn't?

3.   **Day 3:** Practice present-moment mindfulness for 10 minutes.

4.   **Day 4:** Journal: "If I were living my dream life, how would I think today?"

5.   **Day 5:** Create a vision board or write a vivid future script.

6.   **Day 6:** Practice gratitude for your current reality.

7.   **Day 7:** Meditate on your chosen intention. Visualize it unfolding.

Week 2: Vibration & Identity, Embody the Future

1.   **Day 8:** Choose your emotional state today. Use music or movement to embody it.

2.   **Day 9:** Dress and act like the version of you who already has what you want.

3.   **Day 10:** Replace one limiting belief with an empowering one.

4.   **Day 11:** Anchor a positive emotion to a physical gesture (e.g., hand on heart).

5.   **Day 12:** Repeat affirmations in front of the mirror with conviction.

6.   **Day 13:** Visualize success and journal: "What would I do if I already knew it was done?"

7.   **Day 14:** Rest and reflect. Ask: "What identity am I growing into?"

Week 3: Aligned Action, Move as Your Future Self

1.   **Day 15:** Take one bold step you've been avoiding.

2.   **Day 16:** Write and speak only in alignment with your vision.

3.   **Day 17:** Create a mini action plan for one intention. Take step one.

4.   **Day 18:** Identify and shift one habitual pattern that no longer serves you.

5.   **Day 19:** Reach out to someone aligned with your future vision.

6.   **Day 20:** Say no to something that pulls you out of alignment.

7.   **Day 21:** Reflect: How did my actions change when I acted from the future me?

Week 4: Integration & Flow, Let It Become Who You Are

1.   **Day 22:** Practice surrender. Release how and when your goals manifest.

2.   **Day 23:** Walk in nature and observe how ease creates flow.

3.   **Day 24:** Meditate on coherence, aligning heart, mind, and breath.

4.   **Day 25:** Engage in a creative activity without judging the result.

5.   **Day 26:** Journal: "How is the universe supporting me today?"

6.   **Day 27:** Celebrate how far you've come, energetically and physically.

7.   **Day 28:** Write a letter from your future self looking back at today.

8. **Day 29:** Identify your new baseline practices for quantum living.

9. **Day 30:** Commit to 3 quantum habits to carry forward. Integrate them into your lifestyle.

15.3. Quantum Living Habits: Making It a Lifestyle

Lasting transformation comes from integration, not intensity. When quantum practices become habitual, your baseline identity shifts, and your reality keeps up.

Below are high-impact quantum habits to weave into your daily rhythm:

Daily Habits

1. **Morning Reality Sculpting:** Begin each day with intention setting, breathwork, and visualizing your future self.

2. **State Tuning:** Use emotional mastery tools (music, movement, language) to shift your frequency as needed.

3. **Mindful Observation:** Check in with your thoughts mid-day. Redirect focus if needed.

4. **Affirmation Anchoring:** Speak empowering statements while feeling their truth.

5. **Evening Quantum Reflection:** Journal on what aligned today and what you will refine tomorrow.

Weekly Habits

1.   **Identity Audit:** Ask, "Who have I been this week?" and "Who am I choosing to become?"

2.   **Quantum Checkpoint:** Revisit your top intentions. Are you living in coherence with them?

3.   **Energy Reset:** Take one full day each week to rest, unplug, and raise your frequency.

Monthly Habits

1.   **Reality Review:** Reflect on what has shifted and manifested.

2.   **Upgrade Ritual:** Add or remove habits, relationships, and commitments based on alignment.

3.   **Vision Renewal:** Update your vision board, future script, or intention journal.

Quantum living isn't about being perfect, it's about being present, intentional, and energetically aligned.

In the final section, we'll anchor this entire journey with a synthesis of your power, your practice, and your place as the conscious creator of your unfolding reality.

15.4.   Living as the Architect of Your Reality

The purpose of this blueprint is not to overwhelm you with rules, but to empower you with tools, tools that align your inner world with your infinite creative capacity.

You've now explored the fundamental quantum principles of observation, vibration, entanglement, identity, coherence, timelines, potentiality, and transformation. This final chapter is your call to embodiment.

A few final practices to keep close:

1. **Ask daily:** "What reality am I choosing to observe into being today?"

2. **Practice conscious selection:** Choose thoughts, emotions, and actions that serve your highest self.

3. **Stay in motion:** Don't wait for perfect clarity, act in alignment, and the path will appear.

4. **Live from the end:** Feel, think, and move as the version of you who already is, already has, already knows.

You are not chasing a better life, you are becoming the version of yourself who creates it.

With every breath, you are sending instructions to the quantum field. With every thought, you are shaping probability into form. With every aligned action, you are collapsing timelines into destiny.

Live accordingly. Boldly. Consciously. You are the architect of your reality.

This is not just a belief, it is the quantum truth.

Welcome to your new world.

Conclusion: You Are the Embodiment of the Quantum Field

This book has taken you on a journey through the invisible architecture of reality, from the quantum mind to the infinite multiverse, from identity shifts to quantum healing, from the observer effect to superposition and transformation.

And now, it all converges in one essential truth:

You are not simply a participant in the quantum field. You are the field.

Every desire you've ever had, every vision that lights you up, every version of you waiting to be expressed, they're already encoded in the field, awaiting your conscious embodiment.

The blueprint you now hold is more than a 30-day map. It is a lifelong invitation to:

1. Create with clarity.

2. Observe with intention.

3. Embody your future self.

4. Collapse limitations.

5. Expand your frequency.

6. Leap beyond logic.

7. Surrender to flow.

You no longer need to chase outcomes. You are now aligned with the source of creation itself.

As you move forward, keep asking:

1. Who am I being?

2. What reality am I observing into form?

3. What frequency am I transmitting?

Because your answers to these questions will shape not just your experience, but the entire quantum fabric of your life.

So live it. All of it. Consciously. Courageously. Creatively.

You are the embodiment of the quantum field.

And your greatest reality is just one breath, one choice, one intention away.

This is your moment. Make it quantum.

Made in United States
Cleveland, OH
03 June 2025

17474032R00115